Celebrating 25 Years of Calgary Flames Spirit and Hockey History

the Fire Inside

CANWEST
BOOKS

A CANWEST BOOK

A subsidiary of CanWest MediaWorks Publications Inc.

Published by CanWest Books Inc.
A subsidiary of CanWest MediaWorks Publications Inc.
1450 Don Mills Road
Toronto, ON
Canada
M3B 2X7

Library and Archives Canada Cataloguing in Publication

The Calgary Flames : the fire inside / edited by Monica Zurowski. -- Limited ed.

ISBN 1-897229-01-1

1. Calgary Flames (Hockey team)--History. I. Zurowski, Monica

GV848.C28C34 2006   796.962'64'09712338   C2005-906919-8

Published in cooperation with the Calgary Flames and *Calgary Herald*.

Editor: Monica Zurowski
Associate editor: Dale Oviatt
Written by George Johnson, Jean Lefebvre, Scott Cruickshank, Dale Oviatt, Todd Kimberley, Valerie Fortney and Monica Zurowski
Research by Karen Crosby and Andrea Caza
Prepress by Michelle Bowers and Andrew Gilluley

Special thanks to Jim Bagshaw and Laurie Wheeler of the Calgary Flames.

Photos courtesy of the Calgary Flames, *Calgary Herald*, *Edmonton Journal*, *The Province* (Vancouver) and *Vancouver Sun*.
See page 128, which constitutes a continuation of the copyright page, for details.

Book design by John Lightfoot, Lightfoot Art & Design Inc.

Printed and bound in Canada by Friesens

First edition

10 9 8 7 6 5 4 3 2 1

Contents

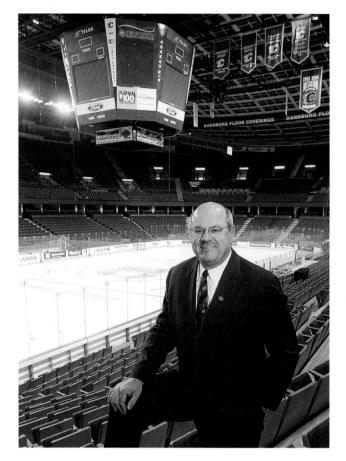

Foreword

Twenty-five years ago a small group of Calgarians had a vision for Calgary's very own NHL team. They took a leap of faith and brought a hockey team from Atlanta to Calgary. The team was christened the Calgary Flames and on Oct. 9, 1980 faced the Quebec Nordiques and played to a 5-5 tie game. A team was born, an instant icon created and a city was smitten.

The ensuing quarter-century has been a blur of memories: a move from the Corral across the street to what is now known as the Pengrowth Saddledome, a Stanley Cup win in 1989, and three battles to the Stanley Cup Finals. The third Stanley Cup run from 2004 is still fresh – it was a spring like no other. That playoff run set the city on fire and unleashed a sea of red that washed over all of us. Tens of thousands of hockey fans rallied behind the Calgary Flames and showed their support any way they could. It was unprecedented; it was overwhelming; it was a city wearing its hockey heart on its sleeve and we will never forget it.

But that was then, and this is now. As we stand on the edge of the next 25 years, we see a new era, a new season and a whole new game before us. If the past is any indication of the future, it promises to be an exciting ride. We thank all of you who have hung on tight and taken this journey with us. We didn't do it alone, and we can't move forward without you. We look forward to painting this town red for a long, long time to come. Here's to the next 25 years!

KEN KING
PRESIDENT & CEO
CALGARY FLAMES HOCKEY CLUB

Foreword

I grew up in St. Albert, just outside Edmonton in Oilers territory. As a kid, I remember the Battle of Alberta and enjoyed the intense rivalry between the two teams. Don't hold it against me, but I have to admit that I was an Oilers fan.

All my friends and family cheered for Edmonton. If anyone had told me back then that one day, I'd be playing in the NHL and playing for the Calgary Flames, I wouldn't have believed it. But that's the thing about life — you just never know what's around the corner. I joined the Flames back in December of 1995 and I've never looked back. It's funny, but it didn't take long to convert my family to being Flames fans. My friends, however, were a tougher sell.

This year we celebrate the Flames' 25th anniversary in Calgary and I feel proud and privileged to be a part of this team and a part of Calgary Flames history. Since the day I arrived, the fans and the city have laid out the welcome mat. In the 10 years that I've been here, that down-home Alberta hospitality has never wavered. It's why I love this team and why I love this town.

There have been lots of ups and downs since I came to Calgary. There were lean years, for sure. Those were the years when all of us on the team just kept grinding it out and trusting that the hard work would pay off eventually. It's amazing, but our fans stuck with us through those tough times and we are very thankful for that support.

Then came the season of 2003-04. How sweet to have that playoff run after such a long dry spell — and what a great feeling to have the fans right there with us. Calgary Flames fans are the best fans anywhere and they proved it to the world that spring. The whole team was absolutely blown away by their support and we felt it every time we hit the ice.

As we mark our 25th anniversary, I'm grateful for all the things this organization and its fans have given me: the highs, the lows, the experiences and the great friendships that have all made me a better person. As we head into our next 25, I can't imagine being anywhere else.

Jarome Iginla
Calgary Flames Hockey Club

flames

6

Passion, Perseverance and the Pursuit of Glory

BY GEORGE JOHNSON

The saga begins, believe it or not, with a cocktail napkin.

The year was 1980 and Vancouver businessman Nelson Skalbania, boarding a flight to Athens, Greece, spotted a small item in the sports section of a newspaper. It said that the NHL's Atlanta Flames were for sale. Intrigued, he called his daughter when his plane landed.

"I told her: 'Take an offer (to buy the team) for a million dollars; get on a plane and go down to Atlanta,'" Skalbania reminisces a quarter-century later. "She was, oh, 17 or 18 years old at the time. Here I (was), lying on a Greek beach, trying to buy a hockey team," Skalbania now laughs, noting he, too, eventually flew to Atlanta, taking $16 million in cash with him to purchase the Flames.

The Flames played their first game in Calgary on Oct. 9, 1980, to a packed house at the Corral. They tied the Quebec Nordiques 5-5.

From that improbable event, the Calgary Flames were born.

"Nelson was on his honeymoon in the Mediterranean, when the idea (to buy the team) came to him," recalls Cliff Fletcher, at the time the general manager at the Omni Coliseum in Atlanta, and now senior vice-president of hockey operations for the Phoenix Coyotes.

"I do remember his daughter sitting in the waiting room outside my office. I knew Nelson, of course, but I had no idea who she was or what she was doing there. And she had the offer on a cocktail napkin! I swear, on a cocktail napkin."

Doc Seaman, B.J. Seaman and Harley Hotchkiss (pictured left to right) were among the original six local businessmen who worked with Nelson Skalbania (far right) to bring the Flames to Calgary.

"The initial purchase came together very quickly," recalls Skalbania, noting that in addition to himself, there was a group of Calgary businessmen interested in bringing the Flames to Calgary. They eventually partnered with Skalbania to buy the Flames, resulting in the team's first ownership group: Skalbania, Harley Hotchkiss, Norm Green, Ralph Scurfield, Normie Kwong, B.J. Seaman and Doc Seaman. (Skalbania would sell his 50 per cent stake in the club to the remaining partners the next year.) "Doc and B.J. Seaman did the leg work on the deal," says Hotchkiss now. "Doc had the idea. He was working closely with (Atlanta owner) Tom Cousins."

Twenty-five years, three Stanley Cup Final appearances and one championship later, Fletcher is probably kicking himself for not stuffing that napkin in a drawer. It would be quite the keepsake. Since relocating from Atlanta to Calgary, the Flames have provided fans with great moments of hockey history. And, the players who have worn the Flames jersey are among the finest of their respective eras.

When the Calgary businessmen first learned that Skalbania was also on the verge of buying the team, they were stunned, Hotchkiss says. "But it was just a bump in the road. Nelson was smart enough to realize that he was out in B.C. and we were here in Calgary, wanting to establish something in our community, (and) give back to grassroots hockey. He needed help. So that's how it all came about."

Fast forward to May 25, 1989: Inside the bedlam of the cramped visiting dressing room at the old Montreal Forum, an infant is dropped on goaltender Mike Vernon's lap, for a cameo keepsake photo. The Stanley Cup is being passed from hand to hand.

"Hey," hollers Vernon good-naturedly, holding the foundling aloft: "This ain't my kid!"

Standing inside a shower stall, with his clothes still on and the water shut off, coach Terry Crisp savoured the moment.

"This is satisfying because the three coaches" — Crisp, assistant coaches Doug Risebrough and Tom Watt — "took 24 players and moulded them into a champion," he said softly. "Gawd, that's something. We took an offensive club and rammed defence into its brain.

"You guys (sports journalists) kept firing me," Crisp said, in reference to criticism the media had directed his way. "But only one man (Flames general manager Cliff Fletcher) had the final say. And that man . . . told me: 'Crispie, forget that garbage. You're my coach.' That meant the world to me."

The team racked up 117 points in that season, 1988-89. There was a nervy Game 7 first-round playoff victory against Vancouver, decided by a Joel Otto overtime goal — or footwedge, depending on your view of the situation. Then, the Flames almost strolled past L.A. and Chicago to reach the penultimate point of any NHL season.

A more emotional, satisfying, history-making finale would be difficult to find. After not making the lineup for the previous game, the iconic Lanny McDonald was thrust back into this one, the final game of the Stanley Cup Finals. He took a pass from teammate Joe Nieuwendyk to score the go-ahead goal. And the indomitable Doug Gilmour, brought out of turmoil in St. Louis and onto the Flames, salted it away by hitting an empty Montreal net with less than 90 seconds left in the game. They were the first invading team to ever lift the Stanley Cup on Forum ice.

Lanny McDonald with the Stanley Cup in 1989.

At the close of the game, Canadiens' fans, classy to the end, stood and applauded the celebrating Flames. A truly magical moment.

"This is the most powerful feeling in hockey," said a jubilant McDonald. "There's no feeling like it. It's something I wish I could describe to people to make them understand how much hard work it takes for 25 guys to put it all together."

Jerseys

The evolution of the Flames jersey:

- *The team is created in Atlanta in 1972, named the Flames and given a flaming A as a symbol, partly in honour of the history of the city, which was deliberately set ablaze during the American Civil War.*

- *After new owners bring the team to Calgary in 1980, they survey the population and fans vote to keep the Flames name over other suggestions, including the Chinooks, Spurs, Cowboys and Mustangs. The flaming A on the jerseys is changed to a flaming C.*

- *The next change entailed adding a touch of black to define the crest.*

- *In 1998, a pedestal of sorts is introduced, on which the flaming C sits.*

- *Celebrating the Year of the Cowboy, the Flames introduce a third jersey before the start of the 1998-99 season — a black jersey with a horse's head, meant to represent "horse power with attitude." The jersey is worn only occasionally over the next season, but eventually becomes the official road jersey, while the team's red jersey is temporarily retired. (The black jersey continues to be an alternate jersey today.)*

- *In October 2003, the Flames unveil their new bold red jerseys, with a black flaming C; it's met with great fan and player approval.*

1972-1979

1980-1994

1995-1998

1998-2000

2001-2003

2003-present

10

Three months later in 1989, Lanny McDonald announced his retirement. He was the player who'd set the team record and scored 66 goals in a Flames season; his moustache had come to symbolize the franchise; and he was always the team's finest ambassador. At a retirement celebration at his home in Springbank, outside Calgary, a tent was set up for the occasion. Tables were garnished with smoked salmon and more strawberries than you'd find on a sunny Sunday afternoon at Wimbledon.

In tribute, left-winger Colin Patterson said at the time: "Sure I remember the first time I met him. How could I forget? My first camp, at the team golf tournament. I didn't know anybody. I mean, who the hell am I? Some free agent out of Clarkson College. Nobody knew me. But who's the first guy I meet? Lanny McDonald. And he comes over and introduces himself to me."

"If I see any new guys at the golf tournaments now, I go right up to them and introduce myself, try to make them feel comfortable, at home. If it isn't too much to ask of Lanny McDonald, it isn't too much to ask of me." Amen.

After retiring as a player, Lanny McDonald would return to the Flames organization in an executive role and then leave again. But what he gave to the city and the team, along with the memories he left, remain indelible.

McDonald hadn't joined the Flames until season No. 2 in Calgary (1981-82), in a trade from the Colorado Rockies. When discussing the history of the Flames, though, what's largely forgotten now in the mists of time is the amazing run up to the Stanley Cup semifinal during the team's first year in town (1980-81), at the old Corral. The team immediately hooked Calgary on NHL hockey.

"I remember our plush offices at the outset — a couple of trailers out in the back at Stampede Park," recalls GM Cliff Fletcher. "It wasn't the lap of luxury right off the bat, but there was an energy and an enthusiasm that really made going to work fun.

"Coming from Atlanta, where we struggled to sell tickets, and moving to Calgary, where we had nothing but sellouts and standing-room-only season tickets, was quite a culture change," says Fletcher.

That first year, forward Kent Nilsson — a flawed genius who could sometimes be hot, and other times not — set franchise standards for points, 131, and assists, 82, that still stand.

"We had a big club," says the coach from that time, Al MacNeil. "A big club. Eric Vail. Ken Houston. Willi Plett. Brad Marsh. Pepper (Jim Peplinski). Phil Russell. And we're playing in this little bandbox, the Corral, with 7,200 seats. Part of the illusion of the Corral was that the boards were five or six inches higher than regulation size. So the sensation for visiting players, in this tiny rink with the high boards, against this huge, physical team and the fans right on top of them . . . well, if you were claustrophobic, you couldn't wait to get the hell out of there."

In the playoffs in 1981, the Flames took out Chicago and then faced the Philadelphia Flyers, who'd just set a record for consecutive games without a loss, 35, the season before. No one gave Calgary a hope in the hereafter, particularly after blowing a chance to eliminate the Flyers on home ice in Game 6.

But, somehow, Calgary pulled the compelling upset, right there at the Spectrum, the hellish shrine of the Flyers, a.k.a. the Broad Street Bullies.

In hindsight, though, this run at the Cup in the spring of '81 is viewed as much as an opportunity missed as a foothold gained.

"That club in Atlanta had never achieved anything," says MacNeil. "Now, (for the Calgary club) to go into Philadelphia and win a Game 7 there was amazing. Amazing."

Many people involved with the Calgary Flames thought just reaching that goal was "enough for now," MacNeil says. "Win a few games and it was 'enough for now.' Score a few goals; it was 'enough for now.' Get far enough in the playoff and it was 'enough for now.' On the plane ride home from Philly (after that Game 7 win), you'd have thought World War II had just ended and Paris was being liberated. These guys thought they'd already won the Stanley Cup. That was on Sunday. Tuesday we opened up against Minnesota in the semifinals. We just gave away the first couple of games, still really pleased with ourselves (because of the earlier victory over Philadelphia), and wound up losing a series (against Minnesota) that we should have won," says MacNeil.

"It was a shame. Because the job wasn't done yet."

The culture of the franchise was in need of a makeover. McDonald arrived the next year, but Nilsson, the Magic Man, hurt a shoulder and the Flames eventually tumbled out of the playoffs in three straight games to the Vancouver Canucks. The next season, Bob Johnson, the irrepressible Badger, was brought in from the University of Wisconsin to coach, and a new era in Flames' hockey had begun.

Bob Johnson. For anyone around during that era, the Badger remains an indelible personality, one of those unforgettable, eccentric people who make, and leave, their mark. The notebooks. The nose-tugging. The irrepressible optimism. A sort of Nutty Professor on ice.

"I just think he loved the game," says tough guy Tim Hunter. "No. Love isn't the proper word. It went beyond love. He had this lust for the game."

A Puppy and Star Is Born!

When the Calgary Flames acquired the first official mascot in NHL history, little did the team know they were acquiring a star that would serve them well for decades to come. Crowds love Harvey the Hound and he loves crowds. Here are a few facts about this crazy canine:

Height: 6 feet, 6 inches.

Weight: 200 pounds.

Born: The lone puppy of a Husky litter in Grant Kelba's Calgary basement on Feb. 16, 1984. That makes him more than 147 years old, in doggy years.

Super skills: Harvey is quite the culinary canine, as he excels in preparing Buffalo Wings, Roast Duck and his personal favourite, Shark Fin Soup.

Rival: S.J. Sharkie from the San Jose Sharks.

Interests: Dog sled racing, howling at the moon (and opposing teams), bird-dogging, water skiing, and walking on glass at the 'Dome.

Records held: The Hound has danced for 18 hours in a dance-a-thon, skied in ski-a-thons, and has climbed all 54 flights and 802 stairs of the Calgary Tower, to raise funds for wildlife.

Famous for: Daredevil antics like walking along the top of the glass rink at the Saddledome, toppling over railings, and not always intentionally, falling off the Zamboni.

Fascinating fact: Harvey the Hound loses 10 pounds of body fluids during every game.

Favourite Movies: *Ace Ventura: Pet Detective, The Incredible Journey.*

Favourite Books: *Hound of the Baskervilles, Don't Shoot the Dog.*

Favourite TV Shows: *Wishbone, Scooby Doo.*

Favourite Songs: "Hound Dog" by Elvis and "Bad to the Bone" by George Thorogood.

Least Favourite incident: Having his tongue ripped out by Edmonton Oiler coach Craig MacTavish in January 2003.

Favourite day: Tongue night at the Saddledome, as thousands of fans cheered on the Calgary Flames with long, red tongues, in honour of Harvey's previous injury.

Special honours: Named the NHL's best mascot by *The Hockey News* magazine in 2003

Challenges were like oxygen to Bob Johnson. He needed them to exist. Up north in Edmonton, Oilers coach Glen Sather had constructed a team of dynastic proportions, a prodigious mountain for Badger Bob to climb.

"He always seemed to dish out the responsibility at the right times to the right people," recalls Hunter, now an assistant coach with the San Jose Sharks. "There were nights he would come to you before the game and say

something like 'Hunter, it's a big game for us and you're going to come through for us tonight. It's a big game and when you play well the whole team plays well. You're an important factor for this team.'

"And then after the game the guys would be sitting around having a beer and we'd find out he told every player the same thing."

13

In 1983, the team moved into its state-of-the-art new home, the Olympic Saddledome. Quietly, Fletcher had begun putting together the building blocks for the core of the '89 championship unit. Al MacInnis and Mike Vernon were drafted in 1981, Gary Roberts and Gary Suter three years later. With a pick obtained from Minnesota in exchange for the enigmatic Nilsson, Joe Nieuwendyk was added. The Flames were the only club willing to take a chance on right-winger Theoren Fleury, a pint-sized jigger of nitro, selecting him 166th overall in 1987. Out of the free-agent U.S. college market, an untapped source of talent up until that time, came Colin Patterson, Joel Otto and Jamie Macoun.

"What helped us," said Coach Johnson, "was having Edmonton just three hours up the road to measure ourselves against. We had the best team in hockey to aim at. So we had no choice but to get better."

That improvement culminated in the shocking 1986 upset of the high-and-mighty Oilers, defending Stanley Cup champions. GM Cliff Fletcher, or Trader Cliff, as he came to be known, had upgraded the talent and competitive level by stealing sniper Joe Mullen from St. Louis. Old Oiler foe John Tonelli was acquired from the New York Islanders in exchange for defenceman Steve Konroyd and winger Rich Kromm.

Most significantly, Calgary-born Mike Vernon was summoned from the minors and provided the Flames with something incumbent No. 1 Reggie Lemelin couldn't — authentic hope to beat Wayne Gretzky, Paul Coffey, Jari Kurri, Glenn Anderson, Mark Messier, Grant Fuhr, and the rest.

Still, no one in their wildest hallucinations could have predicted what would come down in the Smythe Division final. Edmonton, to be honest, seemed all but invincible.

The series boiled down to Game 7 at Northlands Coliseum in Edmonton. Early in the third period, score tied 2-2, rookie Oiler defenceman Steve Smith attempted a cross-ice pass from the side of his own net that hit goalie Grant Fuhr in the left leg and bounced in for the winning goal. Smith was vilified by Edmonton media and fans following the surprising loss. When the Flames arrived home on their charter aircraft, up to 25,000 people had crammed the airport to welcome them.

"I'll cherish that memory, that game, the rest of my life," said Johnson. "That's something they can never take away from me, damnit!"

Sadly, Bob Johnson wouldn't have much longer to live. He died of brain cancer, aged 60, on November 26, 1991. Difficult to accept. Hard to believe. But at least he'd won his Stanley Cup, leading Mario Lemieux and the Pittsburgh Penguins to glory the year before.

The Flames would lose the '86 final, in five games to the Montreal Canadiens. But the ride had been exhilarating, and at the end, with the Cup lost, Calgary fans still stood as one at the Saddledome and chanted, "Thank you, Flames! Thank you, Flames!" for the improbable quest just fallen short.

From '86 to '90, the years were heady ones for the franchise. There were two Presidents' trophies for finishing first in the league. Nieuwendyk would score 51 goals as a rookie in '87 and claim the Calder Trophy as rookie of the year. Hakan Loob became the first European to snipe 50 that same season.

Fletcher also pulled off a coup no one thought possible, negotiating the release of super Soviet Sergei Makarov, the M of the famous KLM line, to play professionally in North America. He paved the way to bring Makarov to Calgary by negotiating a similar move the year before with the unknown Russian player Sergei Priakin. Before Priakin, the Soviet players hadn't been given permission by their country to play in the NHL, but thanks in part to efforts by Fletcher, that rule was changed.

The loquacious Terry Crisp took over as coach to start 1987-88 after Johnson left to run the U.S. hockey program. Calgary would acquire Gilmour by trade that year, and claim its first Presidents' Trophy. A magical season, however, was marred by a four-game sweep by the Edmonton Oilers in the playoffs.

When the next year rolled around, however, the Flames were poised to strike. They'd paid their dues in the embarrassing come-uppance the spring before. At New Year's of '89, 5-foot-6-inch Theo Fleury got called up from the minors. He played half a season, including the playoffs

for the team, embarking on a record-setting tenure with the franchise. All the tumblers were now in place to open the Stanley Cup safe.

"I've always had to accept the fact that I'm small," said Fleury upon his arrival. "There is no changing it. I had to dig down deep, real deep, and say 'Screw the world! There isn't anybody or anything that's going to keep me from reaching my goal.'"

Doug Risebrough, a battle-scarred centreman in the failed '86 Cup run who had graduated to assistant coach, could sense a profound difference in the mindset of this Flames' team.

Oilers defenceman Steve Smith falls to his knees after scoring on his own net during playoff action against the Flames in 1986.

15

"The understanding of going that deep into the playoffs is something you can only acquire by living it," he explains. "It's a huge factor. I'll give you an example. When we went to the finals in '86 in Calgary, the Canadiens threw a big luncheon when the series shifted back to Montreal. They brought out all the heavyweights: Maurice Richard, Jean Beliveau, Yvan Cournoyer. And our guys were just sitting there, mouths open, not even eating, in absolute awe. And I'm thinking: 'Oh, oh. We're screwed.'

"Three years later, same teams, same luncheon. Same heavyweights," says Risebrough. "Only this time our guys didn't even look at them. Finished their meals and they were out of there, because they were focused on the job at hand. Only by getting that far once, do you know how much it hurts to lose. Once you've experienced that, you never want it to happen again," he explains.

Theo Fleury (pictured with teammates above and below) became a mighty offensive force for the Flames throughout the 1990s.

The Flames captured the Cup in '89 and radio play-by-play man Peter Maher's call of "Yeah, baby!" took its place in Calgary lore.

Given the depth of talent on the team and Fletcher's penchant for the deal, Calgary looked set to contend for years to come. But insidious factors were at work, conspiring against that. McDonald retired. Elfin catalyst Hakan Loob went back to Sweden for family reasons. Rob Ramage was shipped out. And early in the 1990-91 season, Jim Peplinski, unhappy with limited playing time, also quit.

Calgary's attempt to recapture the Stanley Cup would crumble the next spring when Mike Krushelnyski scored

in double overtime at the Fabulous Forum in L.A. to oust the defending Cup champs in six games of the opening round. That loss would cost Crisp his job.

Then, on May 16, 1991, Fletcher, the silver fox, the man most responsible for putting together the best team in the game, handed in his resignation. If the Flames were indeed the Rolls Royce of hockey at that time, then Cliff Fletcher was the chauffeur.

"So far," he said back then, "I've heard that I'm resigning because I'm going to Toronto. To New York. To Washington . . . with 50 per cent ownership. Because I'm sick. Because someone in my family is sick. The truth is, I haven't got anything lined up and I feel fine. What I am is stale. Really stale. I turned 55 and I thought to myself, 'I need a career change.' I need to get the old juices flowing again."

It'd take a long time for the Flames organization to recover. Fletcher did, despite his protestations, go to Toronto, stocked up on old Calgary cohorts like Gilmour and Jamie Macoun and Rick Nattress, and commandeered the Leafs to a semifinal appearance against the Gretzky-led L.A. Kings.

The Flames would need 13 years, four changes in the GM's chair and eight different coaches to once again find themselves knocking on the door. Risebrough, having graduated from player to assistant coach to assistant GM, moved into the manager's chair.

But the winds were changing. He would be replaced by Al Coates, who in turn would give way to Craig Button. The decade of the '90s was not kind to the Flames. There were first-round playoff exits to Edmonton, Vancouver, L.A. and San Jose, three of those, cruelly, in a seventh and deciding game. Then came seven years of no playoffs at all. The coaching carousel went round and round: Risebrough begat Guy Charron (for all of 16 games) begat Dave King begat Pierre Page begat Brian Sutter begat Don Hay begat Greg Gilbert.

The new economics of hockey were also taking a toll. Doug Gilmour walked out on New Year's Day 1992 over a contract tiff, triggering a blockbuster 10-player trade with Toronto that in hindsight earned the dubious reputation as *the worst in franchise history*. Star player Joe Nieuwendyk held out for more money and was dealt to Dallas. (In exchange, the Flames got the rights to a largely unknown winger in the Western Hockey League by the name of Jarome Iginla.) Eventually, the Flames couldn't afford Al MacInnis anymore either, and he was shipped to St. Louis in exchange for the estimable Phil Housley. Mike Vernon was sent packing to make way for Trevor Kidd in net. Defenceman Gary Suter was dispatched to San Jose. Left-winger Gary Roberts, plagued by neck injuries, left, too.

In the spring of '99, Fleury, Calgary's only remaining tie to the halcyon days, was dealt to Colorado. The Flames had little choice. The Mighty Mite would've become an unrestricted free agent July 1, and would be seeking between $6 million and $7 million a year.

Team owners in large cities were spending more and more on players' contracts. Once again, the franchise was priced out of the mad hockey market.

The team has varied its logo over the years, but always stayed true to the flame concept created in 1972 in Atlanta.

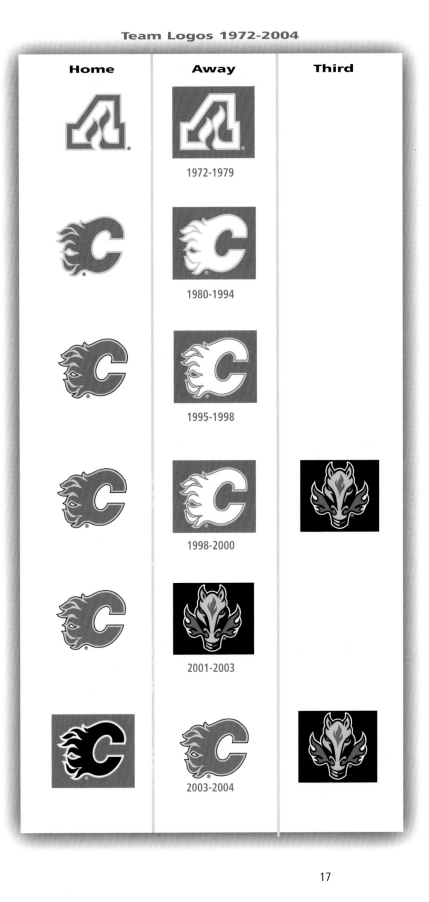

Team Logos 1972-2004

Home	Away	Third
	1972-1979	
	1980-1994	
	1995-1998	
	1998-2000	
	2001-2003	
	2003-2004	

Andrew Ference and Martin Gelinas (right) celebrate Gelinas' overtime winning goal in Game 7 of the playoff series against the Vancouver Canucks in 2004.

"On the surface, when we drafted Fleury," says Al MacNeil, looking back on the decade of unrivalled entertainment he provided, "you're saying to yourself, 'Why the hell waste a pick on this guy?' Then you see him play and your head does 360 degrees on a swivel. He's like Henri Richard. They only brought him into Montreal for a cup of coffee to please his big brother and he stayed 16 years. You couldn't get the puck off him."

Without Fleury, the landscape seemed unbearably bleak.

"For the first 14 years, (owning the team) was fun and successful," says Harley Hotchkiss, who'd taken on the role of chairman of the NHL's board of governors to take the small-market fight to the rest of the league. He undoubtedly became the single most decisive reason the team is still in Calgary.

"Then around 1993-94 it began to change," Hotchkiss says. "How close was it (the team) to leaving? Close. Our attendance went down, our on-ice product wasn't very good. Some people wanted to sell because they didn't believe it would ever make economic sense again. Some owners left, others came on board.

"Those were difficult days, but we hung together." The renaissance for the on-ice fate of the franchise began on Dec. 28, 2002, the day Calgary signed Darryl Sutter as coach, replacing Gilbert after a lengthy search. Fired by San Jose following five seasons of improvement in the Silicon Valley, the Alberta-born Sutter seemed an ideal fit for the Flames. The team was modestly impressive with 19 wins, 18 losses and eight ties under his rule for the rest of the season. But it still marked the first year Sutter had missed the playoffs, as either a player or a coach.

He would not permit that mistake to be repeated. Taking on the arduous dual role of coach/GM, Sutter began to alter the shape of the franchise. He had Jarome Iginla, a

50-goal scorer and undisputed leader of the franchise as his foundation. He brought in silent Finn Miikka Kiprusoff to play goal, a move that proved a brilliant coup. Through 82 games, the Flames battled, overachieved, and propelled forward by Kiprusoff's 1.69 goals-against average and Iginla's 41 snipes, they qualified for the playoffs for the first time since 1995-96.

What happened next will never be forgotten in Calgary — the unparalleled 2004 run to the Stanley Cup Final.

The celebrations were so unexpected and so galvanizing, that they dwarfed anything that had gone on before. The Red Mile along 17th Avenue S.W. had taken over from Electric Avenue as the place to go and kick back after games. Calgary's image had changed almost overnight from an urban cowboy town to party central.

The Flames had succeeded in bringing a city of one million people together, united in a common cause. For sheer dramatics, even London's West End theatre district couldn't rival the drama and excitement. The Martin Gelinas overtime goal to slay the Canucks in Game 7 at the Garage in Vancouver got the ball rolling. Then, they knocked off prohibitively favoured Detroit in six, in front of the delirious faithful at the Pengrowth Saddledome, on yet another Gelinas OT strike.

Goalie Miikka Kiprusoff was on a hot streak throughout the 2004 playoffs.

Team captain Jarome Iginla (right) and the rest of the Flames (below) couldn't hide their disappointment at losing to the Tampa Bay Lightning in Game 7 of the Stanley Cup Final.

The impossible had become the order of the day. So when Sutter's old team, the San Jose Sharks, were the next victims, no one as much as batted an eye. Pre-game introductions at the 'Dome became rites of passage. And the last obstacle to Calgary's second championship was the Tampa Bay Lightning.

The series see-sawed back and forth, fitting for two such evenly matched sides. A Martin St. Louis overtime goal in Game 6 at the 'Dome sent the series back to Florida for a seventh and deciding game.

On that night, June 7, in the sweathouse of the St. Pete Times Forum, the dream ended, just one game and one goal, short. Winners 2-1, the Lightning became the 2003-04 Stanley Cup champions. The Flames had simply run out of gas.

In the aftermath, Iginla sat at his stall in the dressing room, slumped as if hit unexpectedly in the pit of his stomach, trying to make sense of it all.

"We thought that was going to be us out there, hearing that music, listening to the crowd, lifting that Cup," he whispered, eyes a scrappy red, personal feelings on public display. "We wanted to win it for Calgary, our city, the fans who've been so great to us — the best in the league. They showed what a sports city is.

"We wanted to win it for so many reasons. This is going to sit with me for a long time. This is an indescribable sting. This is the worst feeling you can have, the worst I've ever felt, anything I've been a part of. The toughest loss by a thousand times. We worked . . .," his voice trailed off for a moment, ". . . so hard. We got so close." Came so far. Gave so much.

More improbable than '86. More compelling than even '89.

The tears eventually dried and the team began looking forward, as did the fans. With Sutter at the helm, Iginla as the emotional and inspirational wellspring, and Kiprusoff in goal, the future is bright for the Flames. With a new economic order in place, a level playing field for all concerned to work from, the momentum lost from the year-long lockout of 2004-05 is being re-generated.

"I'm optimistic," says owner Hotchkiss. "It was never going to work unless we developed a partnership with the players for the good of the game. Now we have that. There were times that I wondered. We all did. But now we can look to the future and know that if we do our business right, we can be successful and competitive."

As a backdrop, it's not a bad way to kick off the next 25 years of Calgary Flames hockey.

The Calgary Flames 25th season looks bright with goalie Miikka Kiprusoff backstopping a solid team.

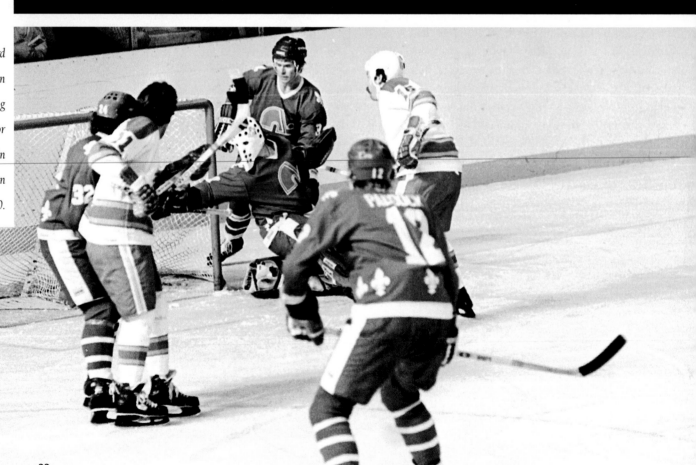

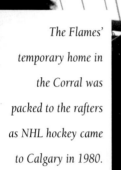

history

The Flames' temporary home in the Corral was packed to the rafters as NHL hockey came to Calgary in 1980.

Guy Chouinard (far right) goes down in history as scoring the first goal ever for the Calgary Flames in their home opener on Oct. 9, 1980.

Twenty-five Years: The Story So Far

Magic Man Kent Nilsson held fans spellbound, as he scored 131 points for the Flames, a team record that still stands a quarter century later.

Big Bucks, Baby!

Not only are the Flames entertaining to watch; they generate a significant economic spinoff throughout the city of Calgary.

From the team's very first game, which was an instant sellout, it became apparent people wanted to spend money on the Flames. Whether it was a $2 program or a $35 jersey, fans were quick to open their wallets in the early '80s. That spending spread throughout the city. Fans visited restaurants and pubs before, during and after the games. Out-of-towners travelled to Calgary to check out the new NHL franchise, booking hotel rooms and doing a bit of shopping along the way.

The economic benefits to the hospitality and retail sectors have grown over the years. And the team's overall economic impact is even larger when you look directly at the Saddledome: The Flames employ 130 to 140 full-time staff who are not players; there are 600 to 800 individuals working on a part-time basis; money is spent at the 'Dome for food, beverages and parking.

About a decade ago, a provincial study indicated the Flames' economic impact to Calgary was between $65 million and $75 million. These days, $75 million to $100 million is a plausible figure, analysts say.

In their first season in Calgary, the Flames did something they'd never done in Atlanta — they won a playoff series. After beating Chicago and then Philadelphia, the team went to the Stanley Cup semifinals against Minnesota.

1980-81

- On May 21, 1980, Flames majority owner Nelson Skalbania announces he and a group of local businessmen have bought the Atlanta Flames and are moving the team to Calgary.
- In July, a deal is struck with the federal, provincial and municipal governments to build the Saddledome — the future home of the Calgary Flames.
- The team's temporary home is the Corral, the smallest arena in the NHL, which brings fans up-close-and-personal with the action, while providing an almost-claustrophobic atmosphere for visiting teams.
- On Oct. 9, 1980, the Flames (under coach Al MacNeil), play their first game in Calgary; the result is a 5-5 tie against Quebec. The Calgary Flames' first-ever goal is scored by Guy Chouinard.
- The Flames' first win comes five days later with a 4-2 victory over Los Angeles.
- Molson Cup winner Kent Nilsson, the Swedish-born forward, is the Flames' superstar of the year, getting the most goals (49), assists (82), and points (131) for the team this season. Those point and assist records still stand as Flames records in 2005-06.
- It's the team's first year in Calgary and to fans' delight, they finish seventh overall in the NHL, making the playoffs. Forward Guy Chouinard garners the most points (17) in playoff action, with centre Bob MacMillan, forward Willi Plett and defenceman Paul Reinhart also making big contributions.
- The Flames defeat Chicago (3-0) in the preliminary round of the playoffs and beat Philadelphia (4-3) in the quarter-finals. Although they lose to Minnesota in the Stanley Cup semifinals (a 4-2 series), Calgarians go wild with excitement and their love affair with the team is born.

1980-81

1981-82

- Meet the Moustache: Alberta boy Lanny McDonald becomes a Flame and nets the most goals (40) for the team this season.
- Most points for the season (87) go to centre Mel Bridgman, while forward Guy Chouinard gets most assists (57) and fellow forward Willi Plett racks up most penalty minutes (288.)
- Goalie Pat Riggin picks up the Molson Cup award, as the Flame who accumulates the most three-star selections during the season.
- Rookie Al MacInnis plays two games for the team, showing a glimmer of his greatness to come. Forward Tim Hunter, one of the team's best-known tough guys, joins, too.
- The Flames, finishing 12th overall, make it into the playoffs, but lose (a 3-0 series) in the Smythe Division semifinals to Vancouver.
- Nelson Skalbania sells his interest in the Flames, leaving ownership in the hands of six Calgary business people. Their aim is not only to provide Calgary with great NHL hockey; they also use the team to promote hockey at all levels throughout the city and to raise millions of dollars for the community.

1981-82

Lanny McDonald's arrival gave the team experience, while his face and famous moustache soon became synonymous with the Flames.

Willi Plett battles Harold Snepsts for the puck in the playoffs, which only lasted one round for the Flames.

Fanning the Flames in the Community

When local businessmen began working at bringing the Flames to Calgary, they wanted to ensure the team was more than a professional sports franchise. The goal was to have a team that was a valuable contributor to the community, impacting the lives of Calgarians in many positive ways.

More than $24 million has flowed from the Flames and the Flames Foundation to charities and worthwhile causes, ranging from hunger and homelessness to literacy, in the team's 25-year history. Those projects — with key contributions from team owners, players, alumni, wives, management and staff — include:
• Ongoing player visits to the Alberta Children's Hospital and the Tom Baker Cancer Centre, where the Flames fund a kids' fun-filled refuge corner.
• A signature project involving a new children's medical initiative announced in the team's silver anniversary season.
• The Calgary Flames Ambassadors program, in which community and business leaders support the Flames and Flames Foundation with fundraising events, including 50/50 draws at home games.
• A reading program for Grade 4, 5 and 6 students that encourages kids to read by rewarding them with Flames bookmarks and player visits to schools.
• The Flames Financial Assistance Program for minor hockey, which helps kids play hockey who otherwise couldn't afford it.
• The Flames also make contributions to worthy causes through the annual Calgary Flames Charity Celebrity Golf Classic; the Danone Superskills Competition; the Community Ticket Program, which allows thousands of less fortunate kids to see a Flames game each year; and Warrener's Corner, a suite for groups of kids hosted by defenceman Rhett Warrener.

TEAM PHOTO **1981-82**

1981-82

Front row: *(left to right) Rejean Lemelin, coach Al MacNeil, assistant general manager David Poile, owners Norman Kwong and Daryl Seaman, president and general manager Cliff Fletcher, owners Harley Hotchkiss, Ralph Scurfield and Norman Green, assistant coach Pierre Page, Pat Riggin.*

Second row: *Trainer Jim (Bearcat) Murray, Kevin LaVallee, Guy Chouinard, Bill Clement, Gary McAdam, captain Phil Russell, Bob Murdoch, Pekka Rautakallio, Jamie Hislop, Denis Cyr, Kent Nilsson, assistant trainer Bobby Stewart.*

Third row: *Paul Reinhart, Mel Bridgman, Steve Konroyd, Pat Ribble, Ken Houston, Willi Plett, Jim Peplinski, Charlie Bourgeois, Ed Beers, Lanny McDonald, Dan Labraaten. Absent: Byron Seaman, owner.*

The offensively charged Oilers, led by Wayne Gretzky, became a huge obstacle in the Flames' playoff path, as Rejean Lemelin experiences here.

1982-83

Doug Risebrough became a new face of the Flames this season and one that would be around for a while, as a player and later as a coach and general manager.

1982-83

● New season, new coach. Bob Johnson takes the reins of the team.

● Bring on the Russians: In an interesting exhibition game, the Flames beat the Soviet National Team 3-2, on Jan. 2, 1983.

● As forward Lanny McDonald finishes his second year as a Flame, he scores a career-high 66 goals — a team record still in existence in 2005-06. McDonald is also selected to the NHL second all-star team; he wins the Molson Cup; and, he's awarded the Bill Masterton Memorial Trophy as the NHL player who best exemplifies the qualities of perseverance, sportsmanship, and dedication to hockey.

● Guy Chouinard makes a mark with the team's highest tally for assists (59) for the season, while Kent Nilsson is still going strong, recording 104 points.

● Forward Doug Risebrough, who eventually will go on to coach the Flames, joins the team.

● The team ranks second in the Smythe Division and 12th overall at the end of the season.

● In playoff action, the Flames defeat Vancouver (3-1) in the Smythe Division semifinals, but lose to Edmonton (4-1) in the Smythe Division finals. It's the first time the two Alberta clubs meet in playoff action and the phenomenon known as the Battle of Alberta begins to grow.

● The Flames' last game in the Corral is played April 18, 1983, ending with a 6-5 loss to Edmonton.

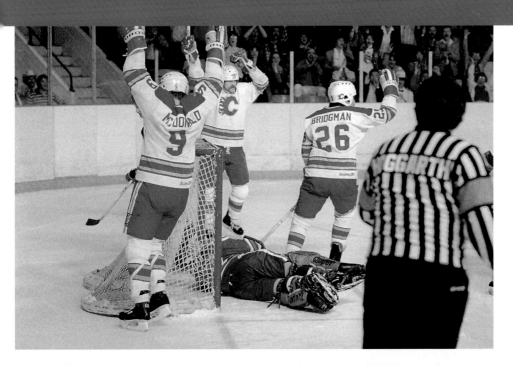

Getting a puck past Oilers super goalie Grant Fuhr was always cause for celebration.

What's in a Number

Lanny McDonald, who set a club record for most goals in a season in 1982-83, always wore the No. 9 jersey when he played with the Flames. When Lanny retired, his jersey number became the only one ever retired by the Flames. (At the direction of the NHL, the number 99 is also retired with the Flames and every other league team, in honour of Wayne Gretzky.)

While the No. 9 is no longer an option for Flames players, jostling for jersey numbers can still be a yearly occurrence. Even Jarome Iginla didn't get his favoured No. 12 when he first joined the team.

Over the years, the jersey number most often chosen in the Flames club is No. 22. Twenty-one different Flames players have worn the number. This includes Willi Plett, who was No. 22 when the team first moved to Calgary from Atlanta; popular centre Craig Conroy (from 2000 to 2004); and the current No. 22, centre Daymond Langkow.

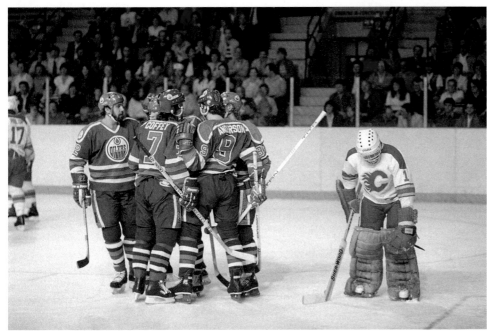

Goalie Don Edwards shows his dejection, as the Flames' last game in the Corral, April 18, 1983, ended with this playoff loss to Edmonton.

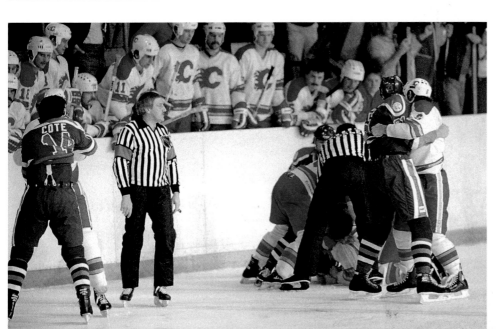

Despite the loss, the playoffs were memorable, as they marked the first time the Flames met the Oilers post-season.

1983-84

- Home sweet home: The Flames move into the Saddledome with their first game held on Oct. 15, 1983; it's a 4-3 loss to Edmonton. Wayne Gretzky and Lanny McDonald take the opening faceoff to officially open the Olympic Saddledome.
- Kent Nilsson is still making his mark as a Calgary Flame, racking up the most points (80) of the season and most assists (49), while forward Eddy Beers takes honours for most goals (36.)
- Forward Hakan Loob and defenceman Jamie Macoun are named NHL rookie all-stars, while goalie Rejean Lemelin is the Molson Cup winner.
- Forward Colin Patterson and centre Dan Quinn start wearing the Flaming C on their chests for the first time.
- At the end of the season, the team finishes second in the Smythe Division and 10th overall.
- In the playoffs, the Flames defeat Vancouver (a 3-1 series) in the division semifinal, but fall to Edmonton (a 4-3 series) in the Smythe Division final. The Battle of Alberta begins to boil.

About 16,700 fans gathered (far right) to cheer on the Flames as they played their first game in the 'Dome, against the Oilers, on Oct. 15, 1983.

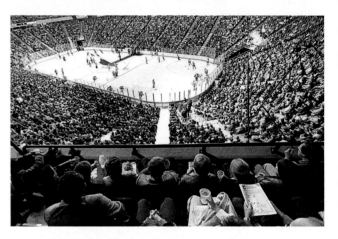

1983-84

Clashes between the two Alberta NHL clubs (such as the one pictured above) provided fast and furious hockey action for fans.

Saddle Up to the 'Dome

- The Saddledome was built between 1981 to 1983, at a cost of $100 million. The province of Alberta and the city of Calgary both contributed $31.5 million, the government of Canada $29.7 million and OCO '88 (the local Olympic organizing committee) provided $5 million.

- The 'Dome's architectural style was unique because of the double curved, hyperbolic paraboloid shell roof. The roof swooped down from a 121-foot high point at its two ends, to a low point of 55 feet at the middle of its two sides. Its saddle shape was designed as a tribute to the area's western heritage.

- At the time of construction, the Saddledome's almost-three-acre roof was the largest free span concrete roof in the world.

- Original interior details: 474,000 square feet, 10 dressing rooms, administration offices, kitchens, medical rooms, TV studio, media lounge, press interview rooms and two darkrooms. The Flames' dressing room had wall-to-wall carpet, weightlifting and exercise equipment, a sauna, whirlpool and a small lounge for watching closed-circuit game films. The Saddledome featured 17,000 padded seats in various shades of green and blue.

- The first 14 rows of seats were retractable, creating an additional 40,000 square feet of floor space. The rink expanded from the NHL's regulation size to the larger ice surface required for International and Olympic hockey. The Olympic Saddledome was the first facility designed for the 1988 Winter Olympics.

- It was built as the principal venue for ice hockey and figure skating during the XV Olympic Winter Games and a permanent home for the Calgary Flames. The building was designed to accommodate large-scale indoor events such as concerts, circuses, trade or agricultural shows, ice and sporting events.

Rookie star Jamie Macoun reacts as the Oilers defeat Calgary and for the second straight year advance to the playoffs over the Flames.

1983-84

The faceoff for the first Flames game in the Saddledome saw NHL President John Ziegler and Calgary Olympic boss Frank King drop the puck between the Oilers' Wayne Gretzky and the Flames' Lanny McDonald.

The Flames were playing hard and fast this season (as Steve Tambellini shows while taking on Doug Lidster), keeping their eyes on the silver chalice they wanted to capture.

1984-85

● Moving on up: The Flames finish the season tied for sixth place overall, breaking team records for goals in a season (363) and points (981.)

● Kent 'Magic Man' Nilsson continues his hockey heroics, earning the most points (99), goals (37) and assists (62) for the team. Hakan Loob nets 37 goals this season, too.

● Goalie Rejean Lemelin wins another Molson Cup.

● Centre Joel Otto takes to the ice in a Flames uniform for the first time.

● Playoff action for the Flames is short and not very sweet this year, as they lose the division semifinal (a 3-1 series) to Winnipeg.

● Co-owner Ralph Scurfield Sr. passes away in February, after a heli-skiing accident.

Captain, Oh My Captain

During the 1984-85 season, Lanny McDonald was making a real mark as captain of the Flames, in terms of leading the team and giving sound advice to younger players.

The role of captain on NHL teams has always been an important one, not only in terms of providing leadership, but also in terms of talking to referees. In 1927, the NHL passed a rule that only allows team captains to address referees, so captains have to know how to keep their cool.

Here are the players who have served as captains of the Calgary Flames.

Jarome Iginla	2003-current
Craig Conroy	2002-2003
Dave Lowry, Bob Boughner and Craig Conroy	2001-2002
Steve Smith and Dave Lowry	2000-2001
Steve Smith	1999-2000
Todd Simpson	1997-1999
Theoren Fleury	1995-1997
Joe Nieuwendyk	1991-1995
Rotating captaincy	1990-1991
Brad McCrimmon	1989-1990
Lanny McDonald and Jim Peplinski	1987-1989
Lanny McDonald, Doug Risebrough and Jim Peplinski	1984-1987
Lanny McDonald and Doug Risebrough	1983-1984
Phil Russell	1981-1983
Brad Marsh	1980-1981

Being taken out of the playoffs in the first round was a blow to the team, but they vowed to come back, more fired up than ever, next season. It's a promise they keep.

Coach Bob Johnson continued to build a team that would soon prove to be Stanley Cup contenders.

1984-85

Flame Doug Risebrough and Oiler Glenn Anderson tango in one of the season's Battle of Alberta matches, which were the hottest events in the province.

1985-86

- Not just another Joe: Forward Joe Mullen is traded to Calgary from St. Louis, tallying 90 points and 44 goals for the year. Other big additions to the team include centre John Tonelli and hometown boy Mike Vernon in goal.
- Defenceman Al MacInnis takes honours for most assists (57) for the team this year. MacInnis and Mullen also each accummulate the most points (19) in the playoffs.
- The Flames again capture sixth place in the NHL and are second in the Smythe Division.
- Defenceman Gary Suter receives the Calder Memorial Trophy for NHL rookie of the year and is named to the NHL rookie all-star team. Hakan Loob wins the Molson Cup.
- As a long playoff run continues, Calgary learns what it's like to be completely gripped by Flames fever, with signs and posters sprouting up on homes and businesses everywhere. Electric Avenue, a downtown strip of bars along 11th Avenue S.W., becomes the gathering place to celebrate victories, with thousands of hooting and hollering fans taking over the street after crucial games.
- So close we can taste it! The Flames win the Smythe Division semifinal over Winnipeg 3-0 and go on to upset Edmonton in Game 7 of the division final on April 30, 1986. Calgarians are ecstatic. That series is followed by victory over St. Louis (4-3) for the Campbell Conference Final. But in the Stanley Cup Finals that follow, the Flames lose against Montreal in Game 5.

1985-86

Players including Gary Suter (above right), Carey Wilson (middle right) and Dan Quinn (bottom right) kept the team's playoff run alive much longer than the previous season's short journey of one round.

32

The Unforgettable Mr. Smith

The night of April 30, 1986, was the occasion of one of the most famous own-goals in NHL history. During Game 7 of the Smythe Division finals between the Flames and the heavily favoured Edmonton Oilers, Edmonton's Steve Smith banked an errant pass off goaltender Grant Fuhr to give the Flames a goal, a lead and eventual win.

"This is the worst feeling I've ever had in my life," defenceman Smith said that day, which was also his 23rd birthday.

For many Flames fans, this gaffe goal became a moment forever synonymous with the name Steve Smith.

Smith, however, continued on in pursuit of a successful hockey career, which ironically ended with him wearing a Flames jersey.

He spent six seasons with the Oilers and was part of three of the club's Stanley Cup champion teams (1987, 1988 and 1990.) Smith then played a further six seasons with the Chicago Blackhawks, which included the honour of being a runner-up for the 1995 Bill Masterton Memorial Trophy for dedication to hockey.

A chronic back condition led to his retirement and in the 1997-98 season he took a job with the Flames as an assistant coach, which he later admitted caused him some apprehension: "I virtually grew up in Edmonton. In a friendly sort of way, you're taught to hate the city of Calgary. I got here and it's 'Wow, I'm with the enemy.' . . . . (But) what's been great about it is the people here have been tremendous to me. From being on the enemy's side, they welcomed me with open arms."

After one season of coaching, Smith decided to make a comeback and played with the Flames during the next three seasons, even becoming the team's captain in 1999-00.

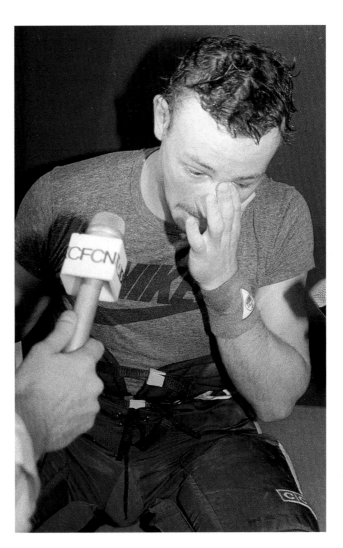

Edmonton Oiler Steve Smith talks to the media after scoring the winning goal for the Calgary Flames into his own net in Game 7 of the Smythe Division finals. It was a pivotal point for the Flames, propelling them forward to their first Stanley Cup Finals.

1985-86

Goalie Mike Vernon became a permanent fixture of the Flames, showing the confidence needed to beat the team's rivals to the north in Edmonton.

33

Flames fever spread as the Calgary squad took their playoff run right to the Stanley Cup Finals.

1985-86

One of the fastest overtime goals in playoff history saw Montreal's Brian Skrudland get one past Mike Vernon in just nine seconds.

The Flames put up a good fight against Montreal in the Stanley Cup Finals, but in the end it wasn't enough.

Fan spirit was everywhere in the city during the playoffs, especially at City Hall where this eight-metre banner hung.

1985-86

Two beautiful banners were hung at the Saddledome at the start of the next season, in honour of the Flames capturing the Smythe Division and Campbell Conference championships in 1985-86.

Lanny McDonald continues to be a key leader, both on and off the ice, even though he tallies 26 points compared to last season's 71.

Doug Risebrough shows the Winnipeg Jets that the Flames won't back down, but the team still comes up short and is eliminated during the first round of the playoffs.

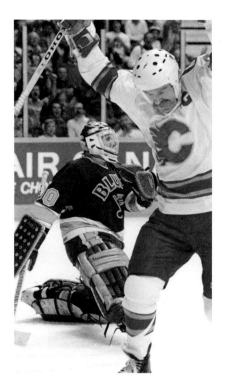

1986-87

1986-87

- They keep getting better: The Flames finish the season in third place overall and second in the Smythe Division.
- Forward Joe Mullen continues to show he's no Joe Average; he gets the most points for the team (87) and most goals (47), while also winning the Molson Cup and Lady Byng Trophy for being the NHL player who displays most gentlemanly conduct.
- Fans are electrified by Al MacInnis's slapshot. He records 20 goals this season, and most assists (56) for the Flames.
- Goalie Mike Vernon starts to really show his stuff this season, with 30 wins.
- Key contributor and tough guy Tim Hunter continues to be a huge presence on ice, racking up 361 penalty minutes during the season. Forward Mike Bullard and left-winger Gary Roberts join the team.
- The Flames make it to the playoffs, but lose to Winnipeg (a 4-2 series) in the division semi-final.

Carey Wilson racks up 51 points for the Flames during the season putting him in the team's top five point-earners with Joe Mullen, Al MacInnis, Paul Reinhart and Mike Bullard.

Mike Bullard has a solid season and scores the most goals (6) for the team during its only playoff series against Winnipeg.

Joe Mullen is the Flames' point leader for the season, showing why coach Badger Bob Johnson wanted him on board so badly.

1986-87

That's Entertainment!

As the Flames became more ingrained in the community, there was a secondary cast of characters associated with the team that the city got to know, including the people who provided some of the voices, music and entertainment that was part of the Flames game experience.

• We stood up whenever Susan Smith entered the room. Despite singing the Canadian and American anthems hundreds and hundreds of times at Flames games, Smith never made a mistake. She became so popular that she got fan mail from across Canada and the U.S.

• You may not hear her voice, but you certainly know her music: Irene Besse was the veteran musician who played the Saddledome organ at the start.

• Grant Kelba was the original 'handler' of mascot Harvey the Hound; he made sure the pup was up for every home game.

• Calgary had the only fiddler in the NHL: Dave Glowasky pleased the crowd with his one-minute bursts of up-tempo fiddle music. His spots alternated with trumpeter Frank Kuhl. The concept for these musicians began with the fans, who'd sometimes bring their own trumpets to the games. In Calgary, the practice originated with a fan named Bill Currie, an electrician who got to be so proficient on his horn that the Flames made him part of the official entertainment in 1986.

• Yeah, baby! It's still the signature call of veteran Flames radio man Peter Maher. The New Brunswick native has been behind the mike for Flames games since 1980. While the other entertainers mentioned above have moved on to other pursuits, Maher's voice still reaches out to fans over radio airwaves.

Terry Crisp tries to motivate the team any way he can after the team loses the opening game of the Smythe Division final to the Edmonton Oilers.

1987-88

Hakan Loob celebrates his 50th goal of the season with Joe Nieuwendyk, who gets his 51st the same night.

1987-88

- Terry Crisp becomes the third coach of the Calgary Flames.
- We're No. 1! The Flames finish first in the league and win the Presidents' Trophy.
- T is for Trophies: Flames players win a number of NHL awards this season, starting with centre Joe Nieuwendyk who scores 51 goals, receives the Calder Memorial Trophy for NHL rookie of the year and is named to the NHL rookie all-star team.
- Lanny McDonald wins the King Clancy Memorial Trophy for leadership and humanitarian contributions. Defenceman Brad McCrimmon receives the Emery Edge Trophy for being the NHL player with the best plus/minus figure in the regular season. Forward Joe Mullen wins the Molson Cup. Hakan Loob on offence and Brad McCrimmon on defence are named to the NHL all-star team, while defenceman Gary Suter is named to the second all-star team.
- On April 3, 1988, Hakan Loob becomes the NHL's first Swede to hit the 50 goal mark.
- Defenceman Rob Ramage and goalie Rick Wamsley become Flames, while Brett Hull and Steve Bozek are traded to St. Louis.
- In playoff action, the Flames defeat Los Angeles (4-1) in the division semifinal, but lose to Edmonton (a 4-0 series) in the Smythe Division final.

Hauling Home the Hardware

The 1987-88 season saw Lanny McDonald winning another NHL trophy, but he's just one of eight Calgary Flames players over the years who have won some prestigious NHL awards.

1. The Maurice 'Rocket' Richard Trophy for most goals: Jarome Iginla in 2003-04 and 2001-02.
2. The Lester B. Pearson Award for being MVP, as voted by players: Jarome Iginla in 2001-02.
3. The Art Ross Trophy for most points: Jarome Iginla in 2001-02.
4. The Bill Masterton Memorial Trophy for dedication: Gary Roberts in 1995-96 and Lanny McDonald in 1982-83.
5. The Calder Memorial Trophy for top rookie: Sergei Makarov in 1989-90, Joe Nieuwendyk in 1987-88 and Gary Suter in 1985-86.
6. The Conn Smythe Trophy for playoff MVP: Al MacInnis in 1988-89.
7. The King Clancy award for commitment to hockey: Jarome Iginla in 2003-04, Joe Nieuwendyk in 1994-95 and Lanny McDonald in 1987-88.
8. The Lady Byng Trophy for gentlemanly conduct: Joe Mullen in 1988-89 and 1986-87.

1987-88

Despite netting 50 points in 52 games, Brett Hull's career in Calgary was cut short with a trade to St. Louis.

The Flames get a few goals in the Smythe Division final, but the Oilers (pictured with the Flames at top and at left) ultimately spoil their party by sweeping the series in four straight games.

39

1988-89

- For the second year in a row, the Flames are the top team at the end of the NHL regular season and win the Presidents' Trophy.
- Forward Joe Mullen gets the most points (110) during the regular season; Mullen and centre Joe Nieuwendyk each get most goals (51); and Mullen and centre Doug Gilmour pick up most assists (59.)
- Nieuwendyk becomes the team's only player to get five goals in one game — Jan. 11, 1989, in Winnipeg.
- Goalie Mike Vernon sizzles with 37 wins, while Tim Hunter sets a Flames all-time record of another kind — most penalty minutes in a season (375.)
- Centre Doug Gilmour joins the team, as does right-winger Theo Fleury.
- Picture-perfect playoffs: The team's playoff run starts with victory over Vancouver (4-3 series) in the division semifinal, followed by a crushing victory over Los Angeles (4-0 series) in the Smythe Division final and then Chicago (4-1 series) in the Campbell Conference final. On to the Stanley Cup Finals, where Calgary beats Montreal (4-2 series) to capture the Cup for the first — and to date, only — time. Yeah, baby!
- It's the first time a road team wins the Stanley Cup against Montreal on the Canadiens' home ice in the Forum.
- Al MacInnis scores the most points (31) in the playoffs and wins the Conn Smythe Trophy for most valuable player in the Stanley Cup playoffs.
- Other awards stream in for Joe Mullen. He receives the Lady Byng for a second time, the Emery Edge for having the best plus/minus figure and the Molson Cup. He's also named to the NHL all-star team, while Al MacInnis and Mike Vernon are appointed to the second team.
- On Aug. 28, 1989, Lanny McDonald announces his retirement.

The Flames were unstoppable this season with many players making huge contributions: Joe Mullen (top) collected 110 points; Lanny McDonald (middle left photo) celebrated his 500th goal; Joe Nieuwendyk (middle right photo) scored a team record five goals in one night; and, tough guy Tim Hunter (bottom) racked up a franchise record of 375 penalty minutes.

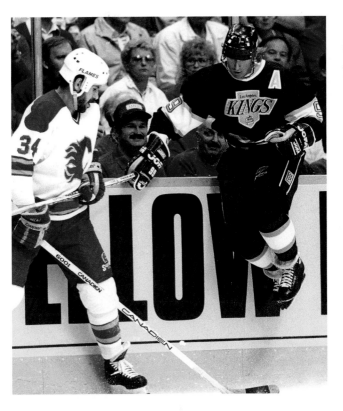

Wayne Gretzky gets out of Jamie Macoun's way in the second round of the playoffs, in which the Flames sweep Los Angeles four games straight for the Smythe Division title.

The Flames bench goes crazy as the team rolls over Chicago four games to one in the Campbell Conference final.

1988-89

Headline of the day: Sea of red floods plaza

From the *Calgary Herald* on May 28, 1989:

The red delirium spread like wildfire through downtown Calgary Saturday, warming the hearts of more than 20,000 cheering Flames fans who endured freezing rain to welcome their heroes home.

The victory parade route along 9th Avenue was jammed four umbrellas deep with hollering spectators, who waved wildly and screamed "Lanny, Lanny" as the flatbed truck bearing the Calgary Flames players wove through the mayhem.

Others bellowed from office windows or threw ticker tape and toilet paper rolls from apartment balconies.

"This is it, what we've all waited for," said jubilant fan Murray Burke, 33.

The parade began at 10 a.m. at Mewata Armories when a police van disgorged its precious cargo — Lord Stanley's Cup — and dozens in the crowd surged forward for a brief touch. A small crane hoisted the Cup into the air to a roar of approval.

Many Calgarians, old hands at attending Stampede parades, arrived hours early to bag a prime viewing spot. Opposite ends of the street passed the time with chanting contests, drowning each other out with hoarse cries of "Who's No. 1?"

When the Flames bandwagon finally arrived, young girls squealed with delight as they dashed into the street and handed flower bouquets to their hockey heart-throbs.

"No one deserves the Stanley Cup more than Lanny, and no team deserves it more than the Flames," declared 62-year-old fan Doreen Erskine.

Children and adults alike swarmed behind the grinning players and followed the caravan faithfully to the Olympic Plaza, where the adrenaline-choked crowd exploded with cheers of "Thank you Flames."

The recipients of all the wild adulation smiled and shivered on the plaza's platform, as the players accepted plaques and handshakes from various rain-soaked dignitaries. The biggest ovation was saved for the team's sentimental favourite.

"We all may be a little cold today, but you have made us warm on the inside," a broken-voiced Lanny McDonald told the fans. "We love you and thank you. Yeah, baby!"

Key contributor Doug Gilmour pumps his arms in the air after Joe Mullen (on the ice) scores Calgary's first goal in Game 3 against Montreal in the Stanley Cup Finals. Calgary eventually captures the series four games to two.

Lanny McDonald celebrates with the crowds in Calgary attending the Stanley Cup victory parade.

1988-89

Calgary's own Mike Vernon holds the Stanley Cup; the Flames become the only visiting team to capture the ultimate hockey prize over the Montreal Canadiens on their home ice.

1988-89

Lanny McDonald enjoys the moment, as he cradles the Stanley Cup after the Flames' big win.

Lanny McDonald announces his retirement before the season starts, but a special ceremony at the 'Dome gives fans one more chance to say goodbye.

1989-90

1989-90

- Training camp sees the Flames go on a road trip to the Soviet Union and Czechoslovakia.
- The Flames end up in first place in the Smythe Division and second place overall at season's end.
- During the season, centre Joe Nieuwendyk scores the most points (95) for the Flames and most goals (45), while fellow centre Doug Gilmour gets most assists (67.)
- The Russians continue to arrive in the NHL, including right winger Sergei Makarov on the Flames. He scoops up the Calder Memorial Trophy for rookie of the year and is selected for the NHL rookie all-star team. But critics question whether the 31-year-old should qualify as a rookie, since he's played with the Soviet Union's best team for years. (Rules are later changed to stipulate a player 26 years of age or older, as of Sept. 15 each season, can't win the Calder.)
- Defenceman Al MacInnis is named to the NHL all-star team and Joe Nieuwendyk wins the Molson Cup.
- Playoff action sees Calgary losing in a 4-2 series to Wayne Gretzky and his team — now the Los Angeles Kings — in the division semifinal.
- On May 18, 1990, former player Doug Risebrough becomes the fourth head coach of the Calgary Flames.
- On June 15, 1990, Norman Green leaves the Flames' ownership group to become owner of the Minnesota (now Dallas) Stars. Green was one of the original six owners — along with B.J. Seaman, Doc Seaman, Harley Hotchkiss, Ralph Scurfield and Norman Kwong — who brought the Flames to Calgary with Nelson Skalbania in 1980.

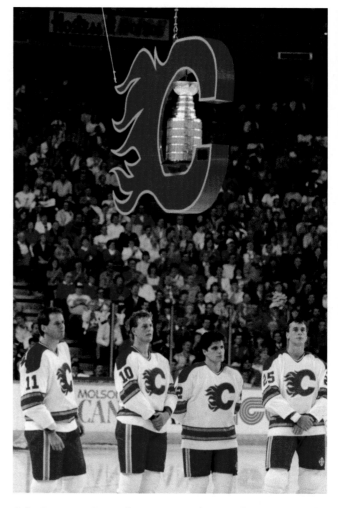

Colin Patterson, Gary Roberts, Sergei Makarov and Joe Nieuwendyk watch as the Stanley Cup is raised to start the new season.

Tim Hunter stands in line for a coffee in Czechoslovakia; the team went there and to the U.S.S.R. for training camp.

What the five-foot-six Theo Fleury lacks in stature, he makes up for in attitude and determination.

The Russians Are Here

For many years, the NHL had enviously eyed the powerhouse hockey players of the Soviet Union, which didn't allow its players to join NHL teams. But that changed in 1989, when the diplomatic efforts of people like Flames general manager Cliff Fletcher began to have an effect. The Soviet Union finally gave permission that year for a select group to play in the NHL.

Fletcher negotiated the first Soviet player into the NHL system — Sergei Priakin, who signed with the Flames in spring 1989. While Priakin didn't have a long NHL career, his arrival opened the door for other Soviets to enter the system starting in 1989-90. These imports included star player Sergei Makarov, who joined the Flames' roster.

Fletcher's work in this area made a large contribution to the NHL and also showcased his ingenuity in building championship teams. Before the Russian conquest, Fletcher had ramped up the search for hockey talent in Europe, leading to acquisitions like Hakan Loob. Under Fletcher, the Flames had also become one of the first teams to sign a significant numbers of players from American colleges, including Jamie Macoun and Joel Otto.

After coming off the win as last season's playoff MVP, Al MacInnis continues to perfect his wicked slapshot. He increases his goal tally from last season's 16 to 28.

1989-90

The Flames, including Joe Mullen (pictured here), mix it up with the Kings in the first round of the playoffs, but lose the series four games to two.

45

Theo Fleury is lightning fast, as seen in this play with the Devils' Ken Daneyko.

1990-91

Among those players who were out with injuries for part of the season were (left to right) Colin Patterson, Dana Murzyn and Paul Ranheim.

Red hot players: Joe Nieuwendyk and Theo Fleury celebrate Nieuwendyk's first goal of the season in a 4-1 victory over Toronto. He'll go to score 45 in the season, while Fleury nets 51.

1990-91

● The Flames are still a powerful force in the NHL, tying for fourth place overall at the end of the season and landing in second place in the Smythe Division.

● Right-winger Theo Fleury captures the honour of scoring the most points (104) for the Flames in the season. It's the first of six times that he'll top the list. He also scores the most goals (51) and wins the Molson Cup.

● Defenceman Al MacInnis has the most assists (75) and is named to the NHL all-star team.

● The Flames make the playoffs, but lose in the first round to Edmonton (in a 4-3 series), after a hard-fought battle.

● In May 1991, Bill Hay is named president and chief executive officer of the Flames, while Doug Risebrough becomes the second Flames general manager.

Bring on the battle: The Flames and the Oilers gave each other a rough ride during the first round of the playoffs, but it was the Oilers who took the series four games to three. Here, Glenn Anderson flies through the air after colliding with the Flames' Frank Musil (top), while the Flames' Ron Stern and Oilers' Adam Graves crash (bottom.)

1990-91

Hello, Hall of Fame

General manager Cliff Fletcher, the man who many called the architect of the Calgary Flames, left the organization at the end of this season and became general manager of the Toronto Maple Leafs.

His contributions to the Flames and the NHL were — and are still today — many, which led to him being elected to the Hockey Hall of Fame as a Builder in 2004. He oversaw the Flames' move from Atlanta to Calgary, where he carefully constructed a team that consistently made it to the playoffs, eventually capturing the Stanley Cup in 1989.

Including Fletcher, there are seven members of the Flames organization who have been inducted into the Hockey Hall of Fame:

• The first Flames player ever honoured in the Hall of Fame was Lanny McDonald, who was inducted Sept. 21, 1992. He played 1,111 NHL games (492 of them with the Flames), racking up 500 goals and 506 assists. He still holds the Flames record for most goals in a season — 66.

• Forward Joe Mullen played 1,062 NHL games (345 with Calgary) and tallied 1,063 points. He was inducted in 2000.

• Inducted in 2003, superstar goalie Grant Fuhr may be best known for his netminding with Edmonton, where he backstopped the team to five Stanley Cups. However, he finished his career with Calgary, where he achieved his 400th career win with the Flames — only the sixth goaltender to reach that mark in NHL history.

• Coach 'Badger' Bob Johnson, loved by fans and players, was inducted in 1992. Well-known for his catch phrase, "It's a great day for hockey," he led the Flames to 193 wins, 52 ties and just 155 losses during his 400-game run with the team.

• Glenn Hall, a goaltending consultant with the Flames from 1988 to 2000, was inducted in 1975 for netminding skills shown during his 18 seasons in the NHL. 'Mr. Goalie,' as he was called, led the league in shutouts for six seasons, including his rookie year, and had his jersey retired by the Chicago Blackhawks.

• Guy Lapointe was an assistant coach and scout with the Flames from 1990-91 to 1998-99, but was inducted into the Hall of Fame in 1993. He was honoured for his 16 NHL seasons with Montreal, St. Louis and Boston; for being a key part of six Stanley-Cup winning teams; and for being part of one of the top defence lines the NHL has ever seen.

1991-92

- Former head coach Bob Johnson dies Nov. 26, 1991. He's inducted into the Hockey Hall of Fame the following year.
- The Flames are fifth in the Smythe Division and 17th overall in a season that sees the performance of left-winger Gary Roberts explode on ice. He captures most points (90) and most goals (53) for the team. It's the second highest total in the team's history.
- Defenceman Al MacInnis nets the most assists (57.)
- Goalie Mike Vernon wins the Molson Cup.
- In a deal that is the subject of many a discussion by hockey fans for years to come, disgruntled Flames star Doug Gilmour is traded to Toronto Maple Leafs as part of a 10-player deal. Along with Gilmour, the Flames say goodbye to defencemen Jamie Macoun and Ric Nattress, centre Kent Manderville and goalie Rick Wamsley. In exchange, coming to the Flames are right-winger Gary Leeman, left-winger Craig Berube, defencemen Alexander Godynyuk and Michel Petit, and goalie Jeff Reese.
- On March 1, 1992, the Flames suffer their most lopsided loss, 11-0 to the Vancouver Canucks at Pacific Coliseum.
- On March 3, 1992, Guy Charron becomes the fifth Flames coach. On May 22 of the same year, he's replaced by Dave King.
- For the first time in 12 seasons, the Calgary Flames miss the playoffs.
- For the first time in the NHL's 75-year history, the players stage a 10-day strike.

1991-92

Gary Suter continues to be part of the backbone of the Flames, but unfortunately the team's dreams are dashed with a less-than-stellar record, which means they don't make it to the playoffs.

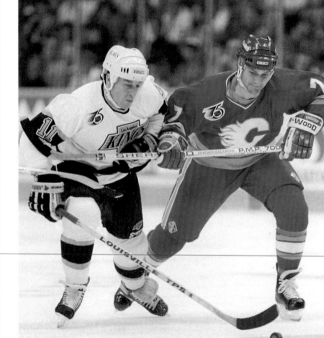

Michel Petit (above) is one of five players who comes to the Flames as part of the 1992 trade that sees Doug Gilmour become a Toronto Maple Leaf.

1992-93

- Lanny McDonald is inducted into Hockey Hall of Fame.
- The Flames finish second in the Smythe Division; ninth overall.
- Right-winger Theo Fleury is a key presence on ice for the Flames. He gets the most points (100) for the team this season, including the most assists (66), while Robert Reichel gets the most goals (40.)

- After a one-year absence from playoff action, the Flames are back, but lose in the first round to Los Angeles (a 4-2 series) in the division semifinal.
- Fleury wins the Molson Cup for the year, and is also a dominant force in the team's short playoff run, getting more points, goals and assists than any other Flame.

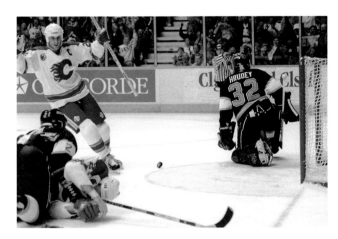

After a one-year absence from the playoffs, the Flames take on the Los Angeles Kings.

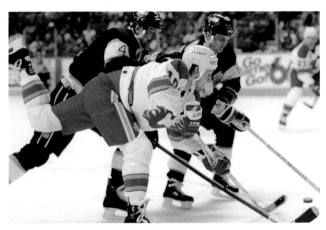

The team wanted to prove to its critics during the playoffs that it was both a decent skating and scoring club.

1992-93

Although the Flames seemed ready to battle L.A., they lost the series four games to two and were bounced from the playoffs after the first round.

In playoff action against Vancouver, the Flames stood up well to several solid hits.

1993-94

1993-94

- A renaming and reorganization of divisions within the NHL leads to the Flames now being in the Pacific Division — and they capture its first ever title, finishing first in their group.
- A variety of players make big contributions to the team during the season: Centre Robert Reichel has the most points (93), left-winger Gary Roberts has the most goals (41), and defenceman Al MacInnis has the most assists (54.) Reichel ties with mighty mite Theo Fleury for second most goals during the season (40.)
- Centre Joe Nieuwendyk wins the Molson Cup, while right-winger Ron Stern captures the title of having the most penalty minutes this season — 243.

- New Flames this season include goalie Trevor Kidd, centres Michael Nylander and German Titov, and defencemen Zarley Zalapski and James Patrick. Those Flames traded away include defenceman Gary Suter and forwards Paul Ranheim and Ted Drury.
- Playoff action sees Calgary losing to Vancouver (a 4-3 series) in the Western Conference quarter-final.
- The Flames assume management of the Saddledome on Aug. 1, 1994. One week later, owners Norman Kwong and Sonia Scurfield leave the team and six new investors are added to the Flames ownership group. The owners plan renovations to the 'Dome and buy the lease from the Calgary Exhibition and Stampede. It costs them $40 million of their own money.

The Flames were enough of an offensive force to take the playoff series against Vancouver all the way to Game 7.

1993-94

Despite fighting for victory in their first series of the playoffs, they ultimately fell short.

Former Flame Sergei Makarov, now of the San Jose Sharks, lays the lumber on Theo Fleury during Game 7 of the Western Conference quarter-finals.

1994-95

1994-95

- The Flames finish first in the Pacific Division for the second year in a row and rank seventh overall in the league.
- NHL teams play a shortened 48-game season due to a 103-day lockout. The deal eventually reached contributes to the problems that small-market teams are suffering, as players' salaries continue to rise.
- Right-winger Theo Fleury again rises to the top of the team, with the most points (58) and most goals (29) for the season. He's named to the NHL's second all-star team.
- Defenceman Phil Housley, playing his first season with the Flames, gets the nod for most assists (35.) He's acquired in a trade with St. Louis for Al MacInnis.

- Goalie Trevor Kidd, who gets 22 wins in the regular season, wins the Molson Cup. Kidd gets a chance to play much more this season, with fellow goalie Mike Vernon being traded to Detroit for defenceman Steve Chiasson.
- Centre Joe Nieuwendyk wins the league's King Clancy Memorial Trophy for leadership and humanitarian contributions.
- The Flames make it to the first round of the playoffs, but lose the Western Conference quarter-finals to San Jose in 4-3 series.

Al MacInnis (right), traded from the Flames, spent time working out in Calgary with his former teammates, including Joel Otto (left), during the lockout this season.

Trevor Kidd celebrates a 5-0 shutout against the San Jose Sharks during the Western Conference quarter-finals. The series, however, went on to a seventh game, which saw the Sharks beat the Flames 5-4 in double overtime.

1994-95

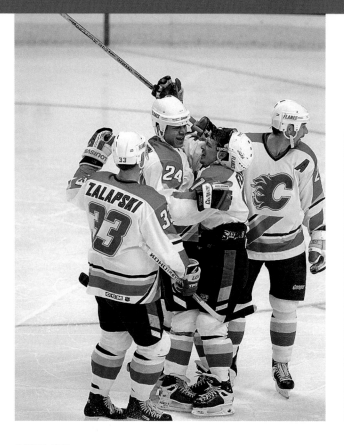

Theo Fleury hugs future star Jarome Iginla (centre), in celebration of Iginla's first goal in the NHL, coming during playoff action against Chicago.

1995-96

1995-96

- In October 1995, the Saddledome reopens, after a $36 million renovation. New seats have been installed, 46 luxury suites have been built (14 rows up from ice level), there's a new President's Club restaurant and lounge, enlarged public concourse, a four TV-screen Jumbotron scoreboard, and 23 new food and beverage concessions. The project was completed by CANA Management Ltd. on time and under budget in 140 days.
- Pierre Page is named the seventh Flames coach, replacing Dave King.

- The Flames finish second in the Pacific Division and tie for 15th overall.
- Theo Fleury dominates, with most goals (46), most assists (50) and most points (96) for the team. He wins the Molson Cup for the year.
- Left-winger Gary Roberts, scoring 22 goals after returning from neck surgery, wins the Bill Masterton Memorial Trophy for perseverance and sportsmanship.
- With economics squeezing small-market teams including the Flames, fan-favourite Joel Otto leaves the team for Philadelphia. During the season, the Flames trade away star-scorer Joe Nieuwendyk for Corey Millen and a still largely unknown junior named Jarome Iginla.
- For the fourth year in a row, the Flames make it to the playoffs, but lose in the first round. This year, they fall to Chicago (a 4-0 series) in the Western Conference quarter-finals. Iginla, however, debuts during the series, scoring one goal and getting one assist.
- It's the last playoff action the Flames will see for eight seasons.
- On May 31, 1996, Ronald Bremner becomes president and CEO of the Flames, while Al Coates is named as the third general manager, taking the reins from Doug Risebrough.

Gary Roberts, shown here battling two Chicago players, stages a remarkable recovery from neck surgery and returns to the Flames, scoring 22 goals along the way.

At the Saddledome, defenceman Zarley Zalapski hauls down former Flames player Joe Nieuwendyk, who was traded to the Dallas Stars during the season.

1996-97

● For the first time in five years, the Flames miss the playoffs, finishing 21st in the league.

● Theo Fleury continues to skate circles around opponents, garnering most goals (29), most assists (38) and most points (67) for the team.

● Flames fans begin the start of a long love affair with Jarome Iginla; he leads all NHL rookies with 50 points and is named to the NHL rookie all-star team.

● Trevor Kidd is the Molson Cup winner; and Mike Sullivan wins the first Ralph T. Scurfield Humanitarian Award for on-ice excellence along with with community service.

● On July 3, 1997, Brian Sutter is named the eighth Flames coach.

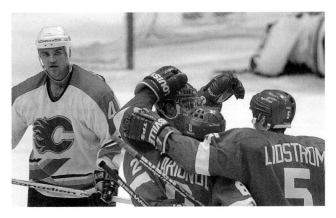

Defenceman Glen Featherstone (left) reacts after Detroit scores a winning goal in overtime during an April 1997 game. Flames players and fans tired of being on the losing end of too many games.

Six Degrees of the Sutter Nation

Brian Sutter was named coach of the Calgary Flames at the end of the 1996-97 season, making one of several connections the famous Sutter family of Viking, Alberta, has with the team.

Brian — along with brothers Darryl, Duane, Brent, Rich and Ron — all played in the NHL, suiting up for a total of 4,994 NHL games, scoring 1,320 goals and notching 2,935 points.

Ron was the only brother to play for the Flames, but Brian took a turn behind the bench (1997-2000), as did Darryl, who started in 2002 and is still head coach and GM today. Ron is also a scout for the team today. And the family legacy continued into the next generation with the Flames drafting Darryl's son Brett and Brian's son Shaun.

"People always wonder how we all turned out so similar in our attitudes," Brent Sutter once mused of the Sutter brothers' phenomenon. "Well, in my mind, there were two reasons: The discipline Mom and Dad instilled in us and the fact there were so many of us. By discipline, I mean getting off the school bus and knowing there were chores that had to be done around the farm. Not thinking of a way to get out of them or finding an excuse to put them off or whining about how unfair it was. Just doing them, whether it meant getting on the tractor out in the fields, feeding the cattle or the pigs, mending a fence . . . whatever. If one of us wasn't around, someone else took on his work. And with so many of us in the family, well, we got used to a team atmosphere very quickly. You had to trust the brother next to you, the same way you have to trust the teammate next to you."

The famous Sutter brothers of Viking, Alberta, go their separate ways in the early 1980s, headed eventually to their various NHL training camps. They are (from left) Darryl, Duane, Ron, Brian, Rich and Brent; Darryl and Brian would go on to become Flames coaches, while Ron became a Flames player and scout.

1996-97

Fans start to get very familiar with seeing Jarome Iginla's face in the sports section of newspapers. He leads all NHL rookies in the scoring race with 50 points.

Theo Fleury, the only remaining player on the team from the 1989 Stanley Cup squad, continues to lead the team as the top scorer.

Todd Simpson, shown here tangling with N.Y. Rangers' Ryan VandenBussche, became captain of the team this season.

Calgary's Juliana Thiessen, then Miss Canada, models the new Flames jersey with Flames players (from left to right) Cale Hulse, Derek Morris, Rocky Thompson and Todd Simpson.

1997-98

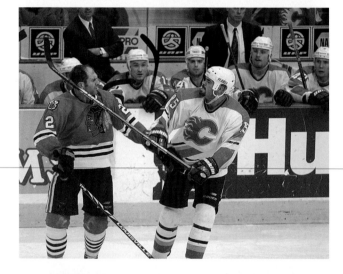

1997-98

- Flames finish 22nd in the league and miss the playoffs.
- Theo Fleury is still a force to be reckoned with: he ties with Cory Stillman for getting most goals (27) for the team this season. He also collects most points (78), most assists (51) and the Molson Cup. Fleury accrues most penalty minutes, too (197.)
- With new coach Brian Sutter behind the bench, the player shuffle continues. New Flames faces this season include right-winger Valeri Bure, centre Jason Wiemer, centre Andrew Cassels and goalie prospect Jean-Sebastien Giguere. Saying goodbye were right-winger Sandy McCarthy, defenceman Zarley Zalapski, left-winger Gary Roberts and goalie Trevor Kidd.
- Defenceman Derek Morris is named to the NHL rookie all-star team and right-winger Ed Ward wins the Scurfield Humanitarian Award.
- In June 1998, the Flames unveil a third jersey in honour of the Year of the Cowboy. The black jersey, meant to represent "horse power with attitude," will be worn only at select games throughout the next season. (After becoming the official road jersey in June 2000, it eventually becomes an alternate jersey in 2003-04.)

Sandy McCarthy (right), shown here taunting Chicago Blackhawks' Eric Weinrich, was a crowd favourite with his tough guy antics. He was traded to Tampa Bay during the season.

Rocky Thompson — skating to the penalty box, following his second fight of the night during a game with the New Jersey Devils — had a short, but memorable appearance with the Flames, largely due to on-ice fights.

1998-99

- The season ends with a 20th place finish for the Flames. For the third year in a row, the team misses the playoffs.
- Centre Cory Stillman offers up the most points (57) for the team, while defenceman Phil Housley gets most assists (43) and Jarome Iginla most goals (28.)
- Goalie Fred Brathwaite wins the Molson Cup, while right-winger Ed Ward captures the Scurfield Humanitarian Award for the second year in a row.
- Theo Fleury becomes the highest scoring Flames player ever, by recording the 823rd point of his career.
- As players' salaries increase and the value of the Canadian dollar plummets, the Flames face increasing financial pressures and decide to trade their biggest star, Theo Fleury. He goes to the Colorado Avalanche on Feb. 28, 1999, with left-winger Chris Dingman, while the Flames get defencemen Wade Belak and prospect Robyn Regehr, along with left-winger Rene Corbet.

The Flames mob Theo Fleury in celebration, as he scores a goal and the 823rd point of his career on Feb. 19, 1999, against the Anaheim Mighty Ducks, setting a new club record and becoming the highest scoring Flame.

Moments like this were too few for the Flames this season: Here, Derek Morris (left) and Phil Housley celebrate Morris's tying goal in the third period of a game with the Los Angeles Kings. The Flames went on to win this one in overtime 5-4.

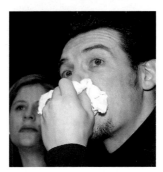

Theo Fleury chokes back emotions and tears at a news conference that announces his trade to the Colorado Avalanche.

1998-99

Ed Ward (left), escaping a scuffle with Vancouver's Mark Messier in this December 1998 game, wins his second Scurfield Humanitarian Award this season for on-ice excellence and community service.

1999-2000

- At the end of the season, the Flames again sit in 20th place, meaning there is no playoff action for the team.
- Right-winger Jarome Iginla is developing and maturing as a player, but the scoring title for the team goes to Valeri Bure, who nets 35 goals and 75 points in the season. Most assists (44) go to defenceman Phil Housley, while goalie Fred Brathwaite tallies most wins (25.)
- Brathwaite wins the Molson Cup, while defenceman Robyn Regehr is awarded the Scurfield Humanitarian Award.
- New names to the Flames roster this season include centre Marc Savard and goalie Grant Fuhr, once a member of the team that Calgary fans believe was public enemy No. 1 — the Edmonton Oilers.
- One of the big stories of the year is the Flames and other Canadian teams struggling against the faltering Canadian dollar. In 1991, the Canadian dollar peaked at 89.3 cents U.S., meaning a $50 million Cdn. budget gave a team in this country $44 million U.S. to work with. In 1999, with the Canadian dollar dropping to 65 cents U.S., that same $50 million budget gives a team only $32.5 million U.S.
- What begins as an inquiry about buying a private box culminates in an oil and gas company purchasing the naming rights to Calgary's Saddledome in June 2000. The hockey arena becomes known as the Pengrowth Saddledome, after a multi-year deal is signed between the Flames and Pengrowth Management Limited's president Jim Kinnear. Kinnear says the company's investment went beyond being a simple business decision: "We feel we're helping to preserve and strengthen an institution that feeds the spirit, the soul, and the very being of this city."

1999-00

Some fans never got used to seeing former Oilers superstar goalie Grant Fuhr in Flames' colours.

Robyn Regehr, shown here in his first home game, joined the Flames and became a crowd favourite.

Val Bure, taking a hit here from St. Louis Blues' Tyson Nash, was a scoring success for the Flames during the season.

The Flames were unsuccessful in blazing a trail to the playoffs, despite opening the season with promise at home against the St. Louis Blues.

Please be seated

This season, attendance at Flames home games hit its lowest level since the team started playing in the Saddledome in 1983-84. But average attendance rebounds down the road and continues to grow in 2005-06, with season tickets again being one of the hottest tickets in town.

Season	Average attendance
1980-81	7,217
1981-82	7,231
1982-83	7,242
1983-84	16,674
1984-85	16,683
1985-86	16,762
1986-87	16,798
1987-88	18,881
1988-89	19,458
1989-90	19,861
1990-91	19,986
1991-92	19,719
1992-93	19,529
1993-94	19,325
1994-95	19,036
1995-96	18,000
1996-97	17,089
1997-98	16,940
1998-99	16,201
1999-00	14,946
2000-01	16,623
2001-02	15,705
2002-03	16,239
2003-04	16,580

Go, Oilers Go?

Disappointment over the Flames' performance in the past few seasons led some people to speculate that hockey fans in Calgary were looking elsewhere for a team to cheer on.

The *Edmonton Journal* had this to say about the state of hockey affairs: "The Flames are such a wretched hockey team that they've done the impossible. They've turned Calgary into a city of Oiler fans. Hockey fans here (in Calgary) are so soured on hockey that they can't even get a good hate going for the Oilers anymore. You see, they have pretty much lost all interest in the game for now. They feel mild support for the Oilers, but only because Edmonton isn't Dallas or Denver or Los Angeles."

Well, it may have been a bleak year, but the bulk of Flames fans hung in there, knowing their loyalty would be rewarded someday soon. Can you say Red Mile?

Mike Vernon returns to his hometown team to finish his career, but Fred Brathwaite gets the call to start between the pipes more often.

2000-01

- With a 20th place finish in the league, the Flames don't make the playoffs.
- Coach Don Hay, who took over from Brian Sutter, is shown the door before the season's over and Greg Gilbert becomes the new coach.
- Right-winger Jarome Iginla begins his run as the team's leader for points (71) and goals (31), while centre Marc Savard picks up most assists (42.)
- The team's two trophies — the Scurfield Humanitarian Award and the Molson Cup — are presented to Iginla.
- Centre Craig Conroy becomes a Flame, as does goalie Mike Vernon, marking his second time in Flames silks.
- Ken King is appointed president and CEO of the Flames in August of 2001, replacing Ron Bremner. King — a big man with a big heart, big voice, and big connections to community and business leaders — works with Flames owners to secure the team's survival in Calgary. Ticket sales, advertising and revenue for the Flames eventually begin a slow upwards climb.
- In 2001, the Flames ownership group buys the interests of two members, Dr. Grant Bartlett and Ronald Joyce. The Flames now have eight local owners who jointly control operations of the Pengrowth Saddledome, the Flames and the Hitmen hockey clubs. The owners are Murray Edwards, Harley Hotchkiss, Alvin Libin, Allan Markin, J.R. (Bud) McCaig, Clayton Riddell, B.J. (Byron) Seaman and Daryl (Doc) Seaman.

2000-01

Craig Conroy joins the Flames this season, destined to become part of a powerful scoring line for the team with Jarome Iginla.

Jason Wiemer, pressuring Sergei Fedorov here, was a big physical presence for the Flames this season, tallying 177 penalty minutes.

2001-02

- At the end of the season, the Flames sit in 22nd place in the NHL and again miss the playoffs.
- A huge bright spot for the team and for fans is Jarome Iginla, who is shooting, scoring and skating his way to fame. Yet again, he's the team's leader in goals (52) and points (96), while linemate Craig Conroy gets the most assists (48.)
- It's a year of hardware heaven for Iggy, as he takes home five awards: the Maurice 'Rocket' Richard Trophy for most goals in the league; the Art Ross Trophy for most points; the Lester B. Pearson Award for being the league's MVP according to players; the Scurfield Humanitarian Award; and the Molson Cup. In addition, he's named to the NHL all-star team and is also a finalist for the Hart Trophy for NHL MVP.
- New Flames this year include centre Rob Niedermayer and goalie Roman Turek, who wins 30 games, becoming the Flames' No. 1 goalie.

2001-02

Roman Turek always stood tall in his role, even in this moment when he lost his stick during a game.

Fans and friends mourned the passing this season of Calgary Flames 'family member' and TV icon Ed Whalen.

Jarome Iginla has become a scoring machine, getting 52 goals — more than any other player in the league this season.

2002-03

- The Flames again finish the season 22nd in the NHL and miss the playoffs for the seventh year in a row.
- There's hope on the horizon, however. Darryl Sutter is hired as coach, replacing Greg Gilbert, and he begins to build a squad that he believes can ultimately win the Stanley Cup. The position of general manager is added to his title in April, 2003.
- Other additions to the Flames include left-winger Martin Gelinas, defenceman Jordan Leopold and centres Chris Drury and Stephane Yelle.
- Throughout the season, right-winger Jarome Iginla gets kudos for obtaining the most points (67), most goals (35) and the Molson Cup. Centre Craig Conroy racks up the most assists (37), while Roman Turek is the goalie with the most wins (27.) Defenceman Robyn Regehr takes home the Scurfield Humanitarian Award.
- During an October game, a streaker — wearing nothing but a pair of red socks — climbs over the glass beside the penalty box and falls nearly three metres onto the ice, smacking the back of his head. The 21-year-old man is unconscious for six minutes and suffers a severe concussion.

He later pleads guilty to a charge of being intoxicated in public and is ordered to pay $2,500 to charities. As the streaker explains, two men had offered him $100 to streak across the 'Dome ice. He thought it would be a good way to help pay for some of his school text books.

Coach got your tongue?

In one of the more memorable moments of the season, Edmonton Oilers head coach Craig MacTavish ripped the tongue out of Flames mascot Harvey the Hound and flung it up into the stands.

MacTavish grabbed the pooch's tongue because Harvey was hanging over the plexiglass by the Oilers' bench, taunting them about the score. At the time of the ruckus, the Flames were ahead 4-0. That lead evaporated as the riled-up Oilers potted three goals in less than four minutes.

Post-game (a 4-3 Flames triumph), Flames president Ken King apologized to the Edmonton visitors for Harvey's antics.

"I would suggest that we had a situation that was intended in the spirit and fun of competition that may have gone just a tad too far," said King.

Much later, MacTavish reflected: "My daughter was a little worried. She wondered if I'd go after Barney (the purple dinosaur)."

2002-03

Darryl Sutter sports a black eye after being struck a few weeks earlier by a deflected puck during a Flames game against Phoenix. He needed minor surgery to repair a nasal fracture.

The Flames hope the addition of new players to the roster, like Chris Drury, will add new life to their playoff drive.

Harvey the Hound stages a triumphant return to the Saddledome, just three days after Oilers coach Craig MacTavish ripped his tongue out.

Martin Gelinas celebrates his winning overtime goal in Game 7 against Vancouver, in the first round of playoff action for the Flames in 2004.

2003-04

2003-04

- The Flames make it to the playoffs for the first time since 1995-96. Fans go crazy, especially as the playoff run continues all the way to the Stanley Cup Finals.
- A new red jersey is introduced as the team's home sweater; sales are so brisk that it becomes one of the NHL's top-selling jersey launches in league history. The popularity of the jersey also leads to a revival of the Sea of Red, or 'C of Red' as some folks call it, at the Saddledome.
- At the end of the regular season, Jarome Iginla leads the team with 73 points, including most goals (41.) He wins the Molson Cup for the year and is named to the NHL's second all-star team. Along with two other NHLers (Ilya Kovalchuk of Atlanta and Rick Nash of Columbus), Iginla also wins the Maurice 'Rocket' Richard Trophy, awarded annually to the player with the most goals scored in a season.
- Centre Craig Conroy has the most assists (39) for the team, while left-winger Chris Simon leads in penalty minutes (250.)

- The Flames make one of the best deals in franchise history and get Miikka Kiprusoff from San Jose, where he was the No. 3 goalie. Despite playing only a partial season for the Flames, and despite a knee injury that sidelines him for six weeks, Kiprusoff nets 24 victories and becomes a huge reason as to why the team makes it to the Cup finals. He establishes a modern-day NHL record with a 1.69 goals-against average and is a finalist for the Vezina Trophy as the league's top goalie.
- In Calgary, the phenomenon known as the Red Mile is born, as tens of thousands of fans gather along 17th Avenue S.W. after every Flames playoff game.
- The playoffs start with the Flames defeating Vancouver four games to three in the Western Conference quarter-finals. They go on to beat Detroit (a 4-2 series) and capture the Western Conference semifinal, followed by victory over San Jose (also a 4-2 series), which gets the team the Western Conference title and a spot in the Stanley Cup Final.

CALGARY VS. VANCOUVER

The Flames were stellar in their first playoff series against Vancouver; here, Miikka Kiprusoff (left) makes a spectacular toe save in Game 7, while Jarome Iginla celebrates (bottom) a goal — one of the 13 he'll net during the Flames playoff run.

● Remarkably, left-winger Martin Gelinas scores the series winning goal in all three of those first playoff rounds. Gelinas is also the year's winner of the Scurfield Humanitarian Award for his perseverance and leadership on ice, combined with dedication to the community.

● The Stanley Cup Finals see the Flames wage a hard-fought battle against the Tampa Bay Lightning. The Flames are on the verge of winning the Cup in Game 6, but a controversial call is made about a possible Flames goal. The shot by Gelinas is ruled a non-goal, although one TV replay shows the puck may have actually gone in the net. Tampa Bay then scores and ends up winning Game 6, which sends both teams to Florida for Game 7. Tampa Bay emerges the victors of that game and Stanley Cup champs with a 2-1 score.

2003-04

Flames delighted fans by taking on, and beating, the Detroit Red Wings in their second playoff series of 2004. Flame player Ville Nieminen (below) tangles with the Red Wings' Nicklas Lidstrom.

2003-04

Red Wings goaltender Curtis Joseph manages to deflect a shot as teammate Mathieu Schneider and the Flames' Marcus Nilson look on.

Jump on the bandwagon; there's always room for one more

Everyone loves a good underdog story — one of those tales where an individual or team is thought to be inferior, but beats the odds and comes out on top. The Calgary Flames, who made it to the Stanley Cup Finals in the 2003-04 season, were one such team.

After sputtering through the early part of the season, the team started coming together. A clever trade saw the team add the goaltending genius of Miikka Kiprusoff into the mix. The team started winning, making the playoffs for the first time in eight seasons.

As the Flames moved through their playoff journey, their fan base widened. Flames fever spread across Canada, with hockey fans making a pilgrimage to Calgary from far and wide to see the miracle of Miikka and the boys on ice. The party zone along 17th Avenue S.W. exploded into a phenomenon called the Red Mile, with up to 60,000 scarlet-clad fans jamming the street after every playoff game. Even politicians got on board. Prime Minister Paul Martin donned a Flames jersey while on a campaign stop in Calgary, dubbing the Flames "Canada's team." Opposition leader Stephen Harper noted he'd owned a Flames jersey for years and surprised on-lookers by winning a Flames trivia contest on a flight to Calgary. (As an aside, he politely declined the prize — a pair of tickets to anywhere Air Canada flies.) And, former prime minister Jean Chretien had lunch with player Martin Gelinas, since both shared the hometown of Shawinigan, Que.

Flames fever was so intense that it was used to motivate the extras in the critically acclaimed *Brokeback Mountain*, filmed in Calgary and area. The extras were told to act like the Flames had just won the Stanley Cup, when the script called for crowds to be overjoyed.

CALGARY VS. DETROIT

After the Flames emerge the victors against Detroit, Red Wings goalie Curtis Joseph congratulates Flames goalie Miikka Kiprusoff (left); Martin Gelinas celebrates with teammates after scoring the winning goal in overtime to beat the Red Wings (top right); Flames captain Jarome Iginla leads his team in the traditional handshake with Detroit (bottom right.)

FACES

Battle-scarred and bearded, the faces of the Calgary Flames became the faces of Canada's hockey heroes as they fought their way through the playoffs.

2003-04

Rhett Warrener

Steve Montador

Mike Commodore

Shean Donovan

Craig Conroy

Ville Nieminen

Robyn Regehr

Dave Lowry

CALGARY VS. SAN JOSE

(Top left) Flames players, including Andrew Ference and Craig Conroy, celebrate their playoff series victory over San Jose at the Pengrowth Saddledome; (top right) Flames captain Jarome Iginla accepts the Clarence S. Campbell Bowl after the game; (bottom left) the Flames' Steve Montador is airbound after being checked by the Sharks' Todd Harvey during the final game; (immediate left) Iginla shouts with joy, as teammate Martin Gelinas gets one past Sharks goalie Evgeni Nabokov.

2003-04

CALGARY VS. TAMPA BAY

Tampa Bay's Cory Stillman and Vincent Lecavalier celebrate a goal in Game 7, one of the rare shots that gets by goalie Miikka Kiprusoff.

2003-04

Players (right) get into a melee during the third period of action in Game 2 in Tampa Bay.

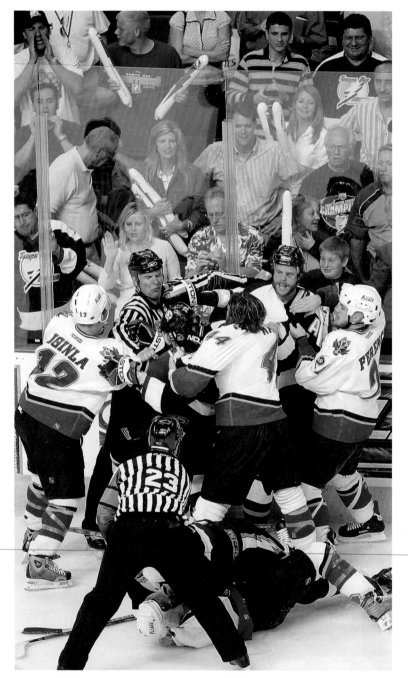

Referees (right) intervene as Jarome Iginla wrestles the Lightning's Vincent Lecavalier to the ground in Game 3.

Miikka Kiprusoff and Ville Nieminen (above) celebrate the Flames' 3-0 victory over the Lightning in Game 3.

Martin Gelinas (above) goes head over heels after an open ice check by the Lightnings' Dave Andreychuk in Game 6.

The Flames would have won the Stanley Cup if this shot by Martin Gelinas in Game 6 (top left) was ruled a goal; (top right) Flames goalie Miikka Kiprusoff make a big save against Lightning player Fredrik Modin in Game 7 against Tampa Bay; (above) Andrew Ference of the Flames hauls down Tampa Bay's Ruslan Fedotenko also in Game 7; (left) the Flames show their disappointment after the Tampa Bay Lightning win the Stanley Cup at the St. Pete Times Forum in Florida.

The ice at the Pengrowth Saddledome was under utilized for much of the 2004-05 season, due to the NHL lockout. Luckily, Calgary still had the Western Hockey League's Hitmen to take to the 'Dome ice and provide hockey entertainment.

2004-05

2004-05

● A 310-day NHL lockout begins, after owners and players are unable to reach a collective bargaining agreement. The entire 2004-05 season passes without any NHL hockey.

● Players spend the season in a variety of ways; most try to stay in shape, some travel, some take the opportunity to spend some quality time with family, and many play hockey in Europe.

● In January 2005, Flames co-owner Bud McCaig passes away suddenly, but peacefully, at the family's vacation home in Barbados. His son Jeffrey McCaig takes his spot in the owners' group later in the year.

● In July 2005, almost 90 per cent of NHL players approve a new collective bargaining agreement with the league.

● The agreement gives teams a $39-million U.S. salary cap, with individual player salaries starting at $450,000 and going up to $7.8 million.

● The NHL also introduces new rules that reward speed and skill. For example, there's to be zero tolerance for obstruction and interference. Goalie equipment is smaller. Goalies have a smaller area to play within. The centre red-line is ignored for purposes of the two-line pass, allowing passes from inside the defensive blue-line to the other team's blue-line. Plus, if a game is not settled in regulation or a five-minute overtime, it will be decided by shootout.

On the final day of operations before the lockout, Flames head coach and GM Darryl Sutter leaves the team's dressing room.

Dean McAmmond (left) and Chris Clark of the Flames share a laugh as they watch from the boards, while taking part in an informal skate with other Flames and local players at the Father David Bauer Arena.

Some Flames players picked up games wherever they could during the lockout. Here, Jason Wiemer takes the opportunity to play hockey in an All-Cal Division II game at the Norma Bush Arena.

Calgary Flames Rhett Warrener manages to tangle up Vancouver Canuck Tyler Bouck as he takes a shot on back-up goalie Philippe Sauve during a game early in the season. After the two teams met in the last playoff run, they've arguably become each other's biggest rivals.

2005-06

● With the lockout now over, every team in the NHL is experiencing a huge shake-up. A new economic structure for teams sees a flood of players changing teams before the season starts. A large number of players have become restricted or unrestricted free agents during the lockout and the teams, including the Calgary Flames, have to figure out who they want.

● In August, the Calgary Flames succeed in doing what every fan wants them to do — they sign their centrepiece player, giving superstar Jarome Iginla a three-year contract worth $21 million U.S. The deal makes Iginla the fifth highest paid player in the NHL. "We've signed the No. 1 free agent in the market," says coach and GM Darryl Sutter. "I don't think there's anybody else who compares."

● Because Iginla signs with the Flames again, Sutter says he's able to attract and keep other players he wants, such as right-winger Tony Amonte who agrees to a two-year, $3.7-million U.S. deal, while another right-winger, Darren McCarty, signs on for a $1.6-million, two-year deal. The Flames also re-sign defenceman Rhett Warrener for four years for $9.4 million U.S.

● Importantly, the Calgary Flames re-sign the man who backstopped them to the Stanley Cup Final last year — Miikka Kiprusoff. He's brought back into the fold via a three-year, $10-million U.S. contract.

● One of several new additions is defenceman Roman Hamrlik, who comes aboard with a reported two-year $7 million U.S. deal. Hamrlik, who was the NHL's No. 1 overall draft pick by Tampa Bay in 1992, played the last four seasons with the New York Islanders.

● Rookie defenceman and Western Hockey League sensation Dion Phaneuf makes his debut with the Flames, earning $942,000 for his first year in the NHL.

● The new team salary cap also means the Flames can't keep a few fan favourites. Craig Conroy and Martin Gelinas, for example, bid adieu.

● Pre-season Flames games are electric, as fans can't wait for their beloved Flames to take to the ice after a one-year break. Ticket sales are red hot, with some games and many season ticket packages sold out before the puck is ever dropped.

● The season starts with the raising of the Western Conference championship banner that the Flames captured in their run for the Stanley Cup in 2004.

● Will the Flames make it to the Cup Finals again this season? Fans hope so, and some analysts believe there's a reasonable chance. *Sports Illustrated*, the American-based weekly magazine, says the Calgary Flames' run at the Stanley Cup in 2004 was no fluke and picks the Flames as the No. 1 team early in the fall.

The Western Conference banner, won by the Flames in 2003-04, is raised at the start of the 2005-06 season.

2005-06

Calgary Flames' Chris Simon (17), Matthew Lombardi (18), Dion Phaneuf and Roman Hamrlik celebrate one of Phaneuf's first NHL goals, shown here playing the Edmonton Oilers.

Records and Rewarding Moments

Open up the record books of the Calgary Flames and you'll find moments to celebrate, moments to cheer and a few moments you might rather forget. But one thing is clear from perusing the team's stats — the Flames' first quarter-century in Calgary has been one wild ride.

Flames' Wins and Losses

SEASON	GAMES PLAYED	WINS	LOSSES	TIES	OT LOSSES	POINTS
2003-04	82	42	30	7	3	94
2002-03	82	29	36	13	4	75
2001-02	82	32	35	12	3	79
2000-01	82	27	36	15	4	73
1999-00	82	31	36	10	5	77
1998-99	82	30	40	12	-	72
1997-98	82	26	41	15	-	67
1996-97	82	32	41	9	-	73
1995-96	82	34	37	11	-	79
1994-95	48	24	17	7	-	55
1993-94	84	42	29	13	-	97
1992-93	84	43	30	11	-	97
1991-92	80	31	37	12	-	74
1990-91	80	46	26	8	-	100
1989-90	80	42	23	15	-	99
1988-89	80	54	17	9	-	117
1987-88	80	48	23	9	-	105
1986-87	80	46	31	3	-	95
1985-86	80	40	31	9	-	89
1984-85	80	41	27	12	-	94
1983-84	80	34	32	14	-	82
1982-83	80	32	34	14	-	78
1981-82	80	29	34	17	-	75
1980-81	80	39	27	14	-	92
1979-80*	80	35	32	13	-	83
1978-79*	80	41	31	8	-	90
1977-78*	80	34	27	19	-	87
1976-77*	80	34	34	12	-	80
1975-76*	80	35	33	12	-	82
1974-75*	80	34	31	15	-	83
1973-74*	78	30	34	14	-	74
1972-73*	78	25	38	15	-	65
TOTALS	**2550**	**1142**	**1010**	**379**	**19**	**2682**

Note: These official Calgary Flames records include seasons from 1972-73 to 1979-80, when the Flames were based in Atlanta.

The Flames achieved the franchise record of 54 wins in one season in 1988-89, including this 4-2 victory (pictured far left) over the Edmonton Oilers on April 2, 1989.

Flames' Playoff Record

Season	Result	Score	Round
2003-04	Defeated Vancouver	4 - 3	Western Conference Quarter-Final
	Defeated Detroit	4 - 2	Western Conference Semi-Final
	Defeated San Jose	4 - 2	Western Conference Final
	Lost to Tampa Bay	3 - 4	Stanley Cup Final
2002-03	Missed Playoffs		
2001-02	Missed Playoffs		
2000-01	Missed Playoffs		
1999-00	Missed Playoffs		
1998-99	Missed Playoffs		
1997-98	Missed Playoffs		
1996-97	Missed Playoffs		
1995-96	Lost to Chicago	0 - 4	Western Conference Quarter-Final
1994-95	Lost to San Jose	3 - 4	Western Conference Quarter-Final
1993-94	Lost to Vancouver	3 - 4	Western Conference Quarter-Final
1992-93	Lost to Los Angeles	2 - 4	Division Semi-Final
1991-92	Missed Playoffs		
1990-91	Lost to Edmonton	3 - 4	Division Semi-Final
1989-90	Lost to Los Angeles	2 - 4	Division Semi-Final
1988-89	Defeated Vancouver	4 - 3	Division Semi-Final
	Defeated Los Angeles	4 - 0	Smythe Division Final
	Defeated Chicago	4 - 1	Campbell Conference Final
	Defeated Montreal	4 - 2	Stanley Cup Final
1987-88	Defeated Los Angeles	4 - 1	Division Semi-Final
	Lost to Edmonton	0 - 4	Smythe Division Final
1986-87	Lost to Winnipeg	2 - 4	Division Semi-Final
1985-86	Defeated Winnipeg	3 - 0	Division Semi-Final
	Defeated Edmonton	4 - 3	Smythe Division Final
	Defeated St. Louis	4 - 3	Campbell Conference Final
	Lost to Montreal	1 - 4	Stanley Cup Final
1984-85	Lost to Winnipeg	1 - 3	Division Semi-Final
1983-84	Defeated Vancouver	3 - 1	Division Semi-Final
	Lost to Edmonton	3 - 4	Smythe Division Final
1982-83	Defeated Vancouver	3 - 1	Division Semi-Final
	Lost to Edmonton	1 - 4	Smythe Division Final
1981-82	Lost to Vancouver	0 - 3	Division Semi-Final
1980-81	Defeated Chicago	3 - 0	Preliminary Round
	Defeated Philadelphia	4 - 3	Quarter-Finals
	Lost to Minnesota	2 - 4	Semi-Finals
1979-80	Lost to NY Rangers	1 - 3	Preliminary Round
1978-79	Lost to Toronto	0 - 2	Preliminary Round
1977-78	Lost to Detroit	0 - 2	Preliminary Round
1976-77	Lost to Los Angeles	1 - 2	Preliminary Round
1975-76	Lost to Los Angeles	0 - 2	Preliminary Round
1974-75	Missed Playoffs		
1973-74	Lost to Philadelphia	0 - 4	Quarter-Finals
1972-73	Missed Playoffs		

After missing the playoffs for seven seasons, the Flames charged all the way to the Stanley Cup Finals in 2004, starting with victory over Vancouver in the Western Conference quarter-final.

Flames All-Time Leaders

Games Played

MacInnis, Al	803
Fleury, Theoren	791
Otto, Joel	730
Peplinski, Jim	711
Iginla, Jarome	626
Suter, Gary	617
Macoun, Jamie	586
Roberts, Gary	585
Nieuwendyk, Joe	577
Hunter, Tim	545
Vail, Eric	539
Vernon, Mike (G)	526
Reinhart, Paul	517
Chouinard, Guy	514
McDonald, Lanny	492
Comeau, Rey	468
Houston, Ken	462
Plett, Willi	452
Loob, Hakan	450
Lysiak, Tom	445
Clement, Bill	444
Nilsson, Kent	425
Reichel, Robert	425
Patterson, Colin	416
Bennett, Curt	405
Bouchard, Dan (G)	398
Stern, Ron	396
Stillman, Cory	393
Gauthier, Denis	384
Manery, Randy	377

Goals

Fleury, Theoren	364
Nieuwendyk, Joe	314
Roberts, Gary	257
Iginla, Jarome	250
Nilsson, Kent	229
McDonald, Lanny	215
MacInnis, Al	213
Vail, Eric	206
Chouinard, Guy	193
Loob, Hakan	193
Mullen, Joe	190
Otto, Joel	167

Points

Fleury, Theoren	830
MacInnis, Al	822
Nieuwendyk, Joe	616
Suter, Gary	565
Nilsson, Kent	562
Chouinard, Guy	529
Roberts, Gary	505
Iginla, Jarome	503
Vail, Eric	452
Reinhart, Paul	444
Lysiak, Tom	431
Loob, Hakan	429

Assists

MacInnis, Al	609
Fleury, Theoren	460
Suter, Gary	437
Chouinard, Guy	336
Reinhart, Paul	335
Nilsson, Kent	333
Nieuwendyk, Joe	302
Lysiak, Tom	276
Peplinski, Jim	263
Otto, Joel	261
Iginla, Jarome	253
Roberts, Gary	248

Penalty Minutes

Hunter, Tim	2405
Roberts, Gary	1736
Otto, Joel	1642
Peplinski, Jim	1467
Fleury, Theoren	1339
Stern, Ron	1288
Plett, Willi	1267
MacInnis, Al	944
Suter, Gary	872
McCarthy, Sandy	730
Sheehy, Neil	725
Macoun, Jamie	664

QUOTABLE AL MACINNIS (NEAR LEFT) ON WINNING THE CONN SMYTHE TROPHY AS THE MVP OF THE PLAYOFFS IN 1989:

"There's no question I feel really happy winning it. (But) if you look down our lineup, there are so many guys that could have won. When you look back at the Vancouver series, Mike Vernon stood on his head for us in overtime. If it weren't for him, we wouldn't be here today. There are guys like Joey Mullen and Joel Otto. The list goes on."

QUOTABLE

JOE NIEUWENDYK ON SCORING FIVE TIMES IN A GAME JAN. 11, 1989:

"I was happy with the five goals. I just didn't want to get any against me."

Hat Tricks and More

Five Goal Game	1
Joe Nieuwendyk	1

Four Goal Games	16
Kent Nilsson	2
Joe Nieuwendyk	2
Joe Mullen	2
Jarome Iginla	1
Keith McCreary	1
Garry Unger	1
Jim Peplinski	1
Hakan Loob	1
Jiri Hrdina	1
Mark Hunter	1
Brian MacLellan	1
Gary Roberts	1
Marc Savard	1

Three Goal Games	154
(Totals include four and five goal games)	
Kent Nilsson	13
Theoren Fleury	13
Joe Nieuwendyk	10
Gary Roberts	10
Lanny McDonald	9
Hakan Loob	6
Eddy Beers	5
Joe Mullen	5
Eric Vail	5
Ken Houston	4
Jarome Iginla	4
Robert Reichel	4
Mark Hunter	3
Bob MacMillan	3
Sergei Makarov	3
Willi Plett	3
Ron Stern	3
Curt Bennett	2
Ivan Boldirev	2
Guy Chouinard	2
Bill Clement	2
Jiri Hrdina	2
Gary McAdam	2
Keith McCreary	2
Joel Otto	2
Marc Savard	2
Cory Stillman	2
German Titov	2
Carey Wilson	2
Valeri Bure	1
Rey Comeau	1
Shean Donovan	1
Barry Gibbs	1
Bobby Gould	1
Brett Hull	1
Dave Kryskow	1
Dan Labraaten	1
Gary Leeman	1
Bob Leiter	1
Matthew Lombardi	1
Tom Lysiak	1
Al MacInnis	1
Brian MacLellan	1
Marty McInnis	1
Dana Murzyn	1
Jim Peplinski	1
Jean Pronovost	1
Paul Ranheim	1
Paul Reinhart	1
Doug Risebrough	1
Larry Romanchych	1
Darcy Rota	1
Claude St. Sauveur	1
Steve Tambellini	1
John Tonelli	1
Gary Unger	1

Flames All Time Top Seasons

Top 10 players with most points in one season

131	Kent Nilsson	1980-81
110	Joe Mullen	1988-89
108	Bob MacMillan	1978-79
107	Guy Chouinard	1978-79
106	Hakan Loob	1987-88
104	Kent Nilsson	1982-83
	Theoren Fleury	1990-91
103	Mike Bullard	1987-88
	Al MacInnis	1990-91
100	Theoren Fleury	1992-93

Top 10 players with most goals in one season

66	Lanny McDonald	1982-83
53	Gary Roberts	1991-92
52	Jarome Iginla	2000-01
51	Theoren Fleury	1990-91
	Joe Mullen	1988-89
	Joe Nieuwendyk	1987-88
	Joe Nieuwendyk	1988-89
50	Guy Chouinard	1978-79
	Hakan Loob	1987-88
49	Kent Nilsson	1980-81

Top 10 players with most assists in one season

82	Kent Nilsson	1980-81
75	Al MacInnis	1990-91
71	Bob MacMillan	1978-79
70	Gary Suter	1987-88
67	Doug Gilmour	1989-90
66	Theoren Fleury	1992-93
62	Al MacInnis	1989-90
	Sergei Makarov	1989-90
	Kent Nilsson	1984-85
61	Doug Gilmour	1990-91

Top 10 players with most penalty minutes in one season

375	Tim Hunter	1988-89
361	Tim Hunter	1986-87
338	Ron Stern	1991-92
337	Tim Hunter	1987-88
291	Tim Hunter	1985-86
288	Willi Plett	1981-82
282	Gary Roberts	1987-88
279	Tim Hunter	1989-90
271	Neil Sheehy	1985-86
259	Tim Hunter	1984-85

Digits at the 'Dome

7: The number of jerseys each player uses during a season. That number includes three home jerseys, three away jerseys and one alternate black jersey. During the 2004 playoffs, each player used an additional two home and two away jerseys.

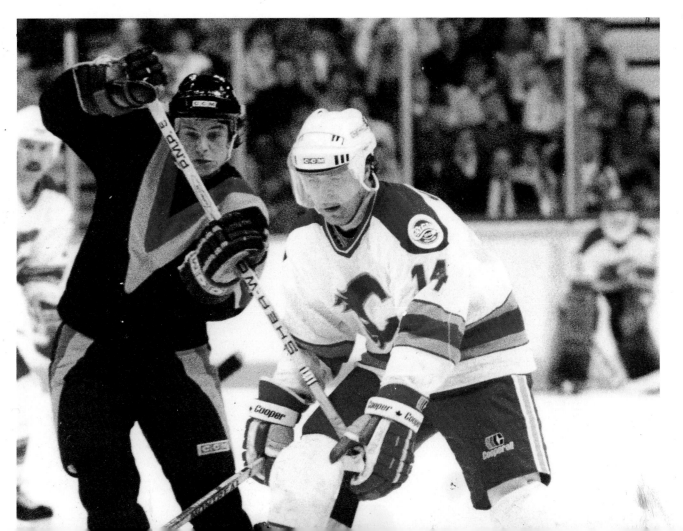

QUOTABLE

KENT NILSSON, WHO STILL HOLDS THE TEAM RECORD FOR MOST POINTS IN A SEASON, ON BEING A FLAME:

"I wouldn't trade life in a team sport for anything. It beats working eight hours a day, that's for sure."

Flames Goalies: In the Crease

FLAMES CAREER GOALTENDERS

GOALTENDER	Games played /	Goals against average
Miikka Kiprusoff	38	1.69
Roman Turek	152	2.53
Ken Wregget	27	2.53
Jamie McLennan	48	2.55
Fred Brathwaite	138	2.54
Rick Tabaracci	97	2.81
Tyler Moss	17	2.81
Trevor Kidd	178	2.83
Dwayne Roloson	70	2.95
Dan Bouchard	398	3.03
J-S Giguere	22	3.07
Andrei Trefilov	22	3.20
Phil Myre	211	3.21
Rick Wamsley	111	3.21
Michael Vernon	526	3.26
Jeff Reese	39	3.39
Marc D'Amour	15	3.43
Dany Sabourin	4	3.55
Rejean Lemelin	324	3.67
Scott Sharples	1	3.69
Jim Craig	4	3.79
Grant Fuhr	23	3.83
Pat Riggin	119	3.88
Steve Guenette	3	4.02
Don Edwards	114	4.06
Yves Belanger	22	4.08
Doug Dadswell	27	4.41
Tim Bernhardt	6	4.50
Tyrone Garner	3	5.18
Jason Muzzatti	2	6.86

Most Wins in a Season

39	Michael Vernon	1987-88
37	Michael Vernon	1988-89
32	Dan Bouchard	1978-79
31	Michael Vernon	1990-91
30	Rejean Lemelin	1984-85
	Roman Turek	2001-02
	Michael Vernon	1986-87
29	Rejean Lemelin	1985-86
	Michael Vernon	1992-93
27	Roman Turek	2002-03
26	Michael Vernon	1993-94
25	Dan Bouchard	1977-78
	Fred Brathwaite	1999-00
24	Michael Vernon	1991-92
	Miikka Kiprusoff	2003-04
23	Dan Bouchard	1979-80
	Michael Vernon	1989-90
22	Trevor Kidd	1994-95
21	Trevor Kidd	1996-97
	Rejean Lemelin	1983-84
	Pat Riggin	1980-81
20	Dan Bouchard	1974-75

Most Losses in a Season

30	Michael Vernon	1991-92
29	Roman Turek	2002-03
28	Roman Turek	2001-02
26	Michael Vernon	1992-93
25	Fred Brathwaite	1999-00
24	Rejean Lemelin	1985-86
23	Trevor Kidd	1996-97
	Phil Myre	1972-73
	Mike Vernon	2000-01
22	Rick Tabaracci	1997-98
21	Dan Bouchard	1978-79
	Trevor Kidd	1995-96
	Michael Vernon	1986-87

* Prior to the 2005-06 season.

Yearly Leaders for the Flames

Season	Goals		Assists		Points		Penalty Minutes	
2003-04	Jarome Iginla	41	Craig Conroy	39	Jarome Iginla	73	Chris Simon	250
2002-03	Jarome Iginla	35	Craig Conroy	37	Jarome Iginla	67	Scott Nichol	149
2001-02	Jarome Iginla	52	Craig Conroy	48	Jarome Iginla	96	Bob Boughner	170
2000-01	Jarome Iginla	31	Marc Savard	42	Jarome Iginla	71	Jason Wiemer	177
1999-00	Valeri Bure	35	Phil Housley	44	Valeri Bure	75	Wade Belak	122
1998-99	Jarome Iginla	28	Phil Housley	43	Cory Stillman	57	Jason Wiemer	177
1997-98	Theoren Fleury	27	Theoren Fleury	51	Theoren Fleury	78	Theoren Fleury	197
	Cory Stillman	27						
1996-97	Theoren Fleury	29	Theoren Fleury	38	Theoren Fleury	67	Todd Simpson	208
1995-96	Theoren Fleury	46	Theoren Fleury	50	Theoren Fleury	96	Sandy McCarthy	173
1994-95	Theoren Fleury	29	Phil Housley	35	Theoren Fleury	58	Ron Stern	163
1993-94	Gary Roberts	41	Al MacInnis	54	Robert Reichel	93	Ron Stern	243
1992-93	Robert Reichel	40	Theoren Fleury	66	Theoren Fleury	100	Craig Berube	209
1991-92	Gary Roberts	53	Al MacInnis	57	Gary Roberts	90	Ron Stern	338
1990-91	Theoren Fleury	51	Al MacInnis	75	Theoren Fleury	104	Gary Roberts	252
1989-90	Joe Nieuwendyk	45	Doug Gilmour	67	Joe Nieuwendyk	95	Tim Hunter	279
1988-89	Joe Nieuwendyk	51	Joe Mullen	59	Joe Mullen	110	Tim Hunter	375
	Joe Mullen	51	Doug Gilmour	59				
1987-88	Joe Nieuwendyk	51	Gary Suter	70	Hakan Loob	106	Tim Hunter	337
1986-87	Joe Mullen	47	Al MacInnis	56	Joe Mullen	87	Tim Hunter	361
1985-86	Hakan Loob	31	Al MacInnis	57	Dan Quinn	72	Tim Hunter	291
1984-85	Nilsson/Loob	37	Kent Nilsson	62	Kent Nilsson	99	Tim Hunter	259
1983-84	Eddy Beers	36	Kent Nilsson	49	Kent Nilsson	80	Paul Baxter	182
1982-83	Lanny McDonald	66	Guy Chouinard	59	Kent Nilsson	104	Doug Risebrough	138
1981-82	Lanny McDonald	34	Guy Chouinard	57	Guy Chouinard	80	Willi Plett	288
1980-81	Kent Nilsson	49	Kent Nilsson	82	Kent Nilsson	131	Willi Plett	239
1979-80	Kent Nilsson	40	Kent Nilsson	53	Kent Nilsson	93	Willi Plett	231
1978-79	Guy Chouinard	50	Bob MacMillan	71	Bob MacMillan	108	Willi Plett	213
1977-78	Bob MacMillan	31	Tom Lysiak	42	Tom Lysiak	69	Willi Plett	171
1976-77	Willi Plett	33	Tom Lysiak	51	Tom Lysiak	81	Willi Plett	123
1975-76	Curt Bennett	34	Tom Lysiak	51	Tom Lysiak	82	Pat Quinn	134
1974-75	Eric Vail	39	Tom Lysiak	52	Tom Lysiak	77	Pat Quinn	156
1973-74	Jacques Richard	27	Tom Lysiak	45	Tom Lysiak	64	Pat Quinn	94
1972-73	Bob Leiter	26	Bob Leiter	34	Bob Leiter	60	Pat Quinn	113

CALGARY FLAMES ALL TIME ROSTER

Player	Seasons	Games Played	Goals	Assists	Points	Penalty Minutes	Jersey No.
Adduono, Rick	1979-80	3	0	0	0	2	17
Ahola, Peter	1993-94	2	0	0	0	2	38
Albelin, Tommy	1995-96 to 2000-01	339	12	59	71	92	5
Allison, Jamie	2001-02	101	3	10	13	163	7, 2, 33
Andersson, Erik	1997-98	12	2	1	3	8	29
Andersson, Niklas	2000-01	11	0	1	1	4	25
Arnason, Chuck	1973-74	33	7	6	13	13	14
Ashton, Brent	1992-93	32	8	11	19	41	15
Bartel, Robin	1985-86	1	0	0	0	0	15
Bassen, Bob	1998-99	41	1	2	3	35	28
Baxter, Paul	1983-84 to 1986-87	209	16	39	55	568	4
Beaudoin, Serge	1979-80	3	0	0	0	0	24
Beers, Eddy	1981-82 to 1985-86	226	87	105	192	232	27
Begin, Steve	1997-98 & 1999-00 to 2002-03	123	11	7	18	192	57, 7, 26, 33
Belak, Wade	1998-99 to 2000-01	72	0	3	3	218	29, 4
Belanger, Yves	1977-78 to 1978-79	22	0	0	0	0	31
Bennett, Curt	1972-73 to 1977-78 & 1979-80	405	126	140	266	190	5,2
Berezan, Perry	1984-85 to 1988-89	152	31	42	73	154	21
Bergqvist, Jonas	1989-90	22	2	5	7	10	18
Bernhardt, Tim	1982-83	6	0	0	0	0	29
Berube, Craig	2001-02 to 2002-03	234	10	17	27	628	23, 16, 27
Betts, Blair	2001-02 to 2003-04	35	3	5	8	12	15
Bialowas, Dwight	1973-74 to 1974-75	48	3	9	12	22	22
Bodak, Bob	1987-88	3	0	0	0	22	28
Boldirev, Ivan	1978-79 to 1979-80	65	22	32	54	26	12
Bolduc, Dan	1983-84	2	0	1	1	0	32
Borschevsky, Nikolai	1994-95	8	0	5	5	7	16
Botterill, Jason	1999-00 & 2001-02	6	1	0	1	2	17, 20
Botting, Cam	1975-76	2	0	1	1	0	24
Bouchard, Dan	1972-73 to 1980-81	398	0	16	16	146	30
Bouchard, Joel	1994-95 to 1997-98	126	9	12	21	106	34, 5, 6
Boughner, Bob	2001-02 to 2002-03	148	5	18	23	293	6
Bourgeois, Charles	1981-82 to 1985-86	162	12	34	46	430	2, 28
Bowness, Rick	1975-76 to 1976-77	33	0	4	4	29	15
Bozek, Steve	1983-84 to 1987-88	261	64	79	143	80	26
Bradley, Brian	1985-86 to 1987-88	45	10	19	29	16	14
Brathwaite, Fred	1998-99 to 2000-01	138	0	3	3	45	40
Bridgman, Mel	1981-82 to 1982-83	142	45	80	125	197	26
Brigley, Travis	1997-98 & 1999-00	19	0	2	2	6	43, 26
Brochu, Martin	2000-01	0	0	0	0	0	30
Brown, Arnie	1972-73 to 1973-74	63	3	6	9	46	19
Brubaker, Jeff	1983-84	4	0	0	0	19	29
Bucyk, Randy	1987-88	2	0	0	0	0	18
Bullard, Mike	1986-87 to 1987-88	136	76	81	157	102	22, 25
Bure, Valeri	1997-98 to 2000-01	256	93	99	192	100	8
Bureau, Marc	1989-90 to 1990-91 & 1999-00	19	1	3	4	8	33, 7
Buzek, Petr	2001-02 to 2002-03	76	4	8	12	28	8
Byers, Jerry	1974-75	12	1	1	2	9	10
Carr, Gene	1978-79	30	3	8	11	6	14
Carriere, Larry	1975-76 to 1976-77	100	6	18	24	112	23
Cassels, Andrew	1997-98 to 1998-99	151	29	52	81	50	21
Cavallini, Gino	1984-85 to 1985-86	54	13	17	30	40	6
Charron, Eric	1997-98 to 1999-00	35	0	1	1	55	38, 36
Chernomaz, Richard	1987-88 to 1988-89 &1991-92	14	1	0	1	6	15, 33, 16
Chiasson, Steve	1994-95 to 1996-97	168	15	59	74	133	21
Chorske, Tom	1998-99	7	0	0	0	2	26
Chouinard, Guy	1974-75 to 1982-83	514	193	336	529	110	10, 16, 7

Player	Seasons	Games Played	Goals	Assists	Points	Penalty Minutes	Jersey No.
Christie, Ryan	2001-02	2	0	0	0	0	39
Christoff, Steve	1982-83	45	9	8	17	4	11
Churla, Shane	1987-88 to 1988-89	34	1	5	6	158	15
Clark, Chris	1999-00 to 2003-04	278	35	36	71	363	7, 17, 26
Clement, Bill	1975-76 to 1981-82	444	85	139	224	197	10
Comeau, Rey	1972-73 to 1977-78	468	88	126	214	153	18
Commodore, Mike	2002-03 to 2003-04	18	0	1	1	44	2
Conacher, Pat	1995-96	7	0	0	0	0	11
Conroy, Craig	2000-02 to 2003-04	237	60	128	188	126	22
Corbet, Rene	1998-99 to 1999-00	68	9	14	23	70	20
Courteau, Yves	1984-85	18	2	5	7	4	25
Cowan, Jeff	1999-00 to 2001-02	83	14	5	19	130	38
Coxe, Craig	1987-88	7	2	3	5	32	18
Craig, Jim	1979-80	4	0	0	0	0	1
Curtale, Tony	1980-81	2	0	0	0	0	3
Cyr, Denis	1980-81 to 1982-83	66	14	15	29	13	9, 12
D'Amour, Marc	1985-86	16	0	0	0	22	1
Dadswell, Doug	1986-87 to 1987-88	27	0	2	2	2	36
Dahl, Kevin	1992-93 to 1995-96 & 1997-98	179	7	22	29	149	4
Dahlquist, Chris	1992-93 to 1993-94	151	4	18	22	118	5
Deadmarsh, Butch	1972-73 to 1973-74	61	7	1	8	97	10
DeGray, Dale	1985-86 to 1986-87	28	6	7	13	29	28
Dingman, Chris	1997-98 to 1998-99	72	3	3	6	166	7
Dollas, Bobby	1999-00	49	3	7	10	28	4
Dome, Robert	2002-03	1	0	0	0	0	38
Domenichelli, Hnat	1996-97 to 1999-00	96	20	23	43	31	17
Donovan, Shean	2002-03 to 2003-04	95	19	26	45	79	16
Dowd, Jim	1997-98	48	6	8	14	12	34
Dubinsky, Steve	1998-99 to 1999-00	84	4	11	15	18	18
Drury, Chris	2002-03	80	23	30	53	33	37, 18
Drury, Ted	1993-94	34	5	7	12	26	27
Dunn, Richie	1982-83	80	3	11	14	47	6
DuPont, Micki	2001-02 to 2002-03	18	1	2	3	6	42
Dwyer, Mike	1980-81 to 1981-82	9	0	3	3	4	29, 26
Eakin, Bruce	1981-82 & 1983-84 to 1984-85	9	2	1	3	4	19, 22. 25, 32
Eakins, Dallas	2000-01 to 2001-02	20	0	1	1	15	4, 20, 26
Eaves, Mike	1983-84 to 1985-86	117	28	65	93	30	7, 17
Ecclestone, Tim	1974-75 to 1977-78	220	28	62	90	92	14
Edwards, Don	1982-83 to 1984-85	114	0	3	3	6	1
Eisenhut, Neil	1994-95	3	0	0	0	0	35
Eloranta, Kari	1981-82 to 1984-85 & 1985-86	255	12	96	108	149	8, 20, 32
Engblom, Brian	1986-87	32	0	4	4	28	6
Esau, Len	1993-94 to 1994-95	7	0	3	3	7	36, 28
Evans, Brennan	2003-04	2 playoff games					43
Evason, Dean	1995-96	67	7	7	14	38	20
Fata, Rico	1998-99 to 2000-01	27	0	1	1	10	62, 44, 15
Featerstone, Glen	1996-97	13	1	3	4	19	4
Fenton, Paul	1990-91	31	5	7	12	10	12
Ference, Andrew	2002-03 to 2003-04	88	4	16	20	59	21
Ferguson, Craig	1995-96	8	0	0	0	4	38
Flett, Bill	1975-76 to 1976-77	102	27	21	48	36	9
Fleury, Theoren	1988-89 to 1998-99	791	364	466	830	1339	14
Forslund, Tomas	1991-92 to 1992-93	44	5	11	16	12	27
Fotiu, Nick	1985-86 to 1986-87	51	5	4	9	166	22
Fox, Greg	1977-78 to 1978-79	80	1	14	15	95	2
Freer, Mark	1993-94	2	0	0	0	4	16
Fuhr, Grant	1999-00	23	0	0	0	2	31

Digits at the 'Dome

6: The age Jarome Iginla was when he first picked up a hockey stick and laced up a pair of skates. As a boy, he played goalie for two years before switching over to forward.

QUOTABLE
CRAIG CONROY ON
LEAVING THE FLAMES:
"It was tough
(to leave) because
we had such a great run.
I would have loved to
have stayed. I said that
and I meant that, but I
had to do what was best
for me and my family."

QUOTABLE

DOUG GILMOUR ON LEAVING THE FLAMES:

"It's the biggest move I've ever made in my career. Whether it was right or wrong, I cannot tell you that. But it's something I believe had to be done."

Player	Seasons	Games Played	Goals	Assists	Points	Penalty Minutes	Jersey No.
Gagner, Dave	1996-97	82	27	33	60	48	51
Garner, Tyrone	1997-98 to 1998-99	3	0	0	0	0	37, 1
Gauthier, Denis	1997-98 to 2003-04	384	13	45	58	515	24, 3
Gavey, Aaron	1996-97 to 1997-98	67	9	12	21	58	23
Gelinas, Martin	2002-03 to 2003-04	157	38	49	87	121	23
Gibbs, Barry	1974-75 to 1977-78	208	13	55	68	218	2
Giguere, Jean-Sebastien	1998-99 to 1999-00	22	0	1	1	6	47
Gilmour, Doug	1988-89 to 1991-92	266	81	214	295	286	39
Glynn, Brian	1987-88 & 1989-90	68	5	14	19	87	32
Godynyuk, Alexander	1991-92 to 1992-93	33	3	5	8	23	21
Gorman, Dave	1979-80	3	0	0	0	0	15
Gould, Bob	1979-80 to 1981-82	20	3	0	3	4	22, 19
Gould, John	1976-77 to 1978-79	194	35	50	85	47	21
Gratton, Benoit	1999-00 to 2000-01	24	1	5	6	24	37, 39
Gratton, Norm	1972-73	29	3	6	9	12	10
Graves, Hilliard	1974-75 to 1976-77	172	37	54	91	63	17
Green, Josh	2003-04	36	2	4	6	24	26
Greig, Mark	1994-95	8	1	1	2	2	16
Grimson, Stu	1988-89 to 1989-90	4	0	0	0	22	18, 35
Guenette, Steve	1989-90 to 1990-91	3	0	0	0	2	1
Guy, Kevan	1986-87 to 1987-88 & 1990-91 to 1991-92	42	0	7	7	33	3, 5
Haas, David	1993-94	2	1	1	2	7	19
Habscheid, Marc	1991-92	46	7	11	18	42	17
Hampson, Gord	1982-83	4	0	0	0	5	27
Hanson, Keith	1983-84	25	0	2	2	77	6
Harkins, Todd	1991-92 to 1992-93	20	2	3	5	29	37, 19
Harrer, Tim	1982-83	3	0	0	0	2	12
Harris, Ron	1972-73	24	2	4	6	8	5
Harvey, Buster	1974-75 to 1975-76	80	17	27	44	16	8
Hay, Dwayne	2000-01	49	1	3	4	16	21
Heaphy, Shawn	1992-93	1	0	0	0	0	13
Helenius, Sami	1996-97 & 1998-99	7	0	1	1	8	8, 4
Henderson, Paul	1979-80	30	7	6	13	6	15, 19
Hentunen, Jukka	2001-02	28	2	3	5	4	24
Hextall, Bryan	1973-74 to 1974-75	114	20	20	40	117	20
Hicke, Ernie	1972-73	58	14	23	37	37	12
Hindmarch, Dave	1980-81 to 1984-85	98	21	17	38	25	18
Hislop, Jamie	1980-81 to 1983-84	215	37	61	98	65	17
Hlushko, Todd	1994-95 to 1997-98	76	7	13	20	84	38, 17, 20
Hoglund, Jonas	1996-97 to 1997-98	118	25	24	49	28	44
Hogoboam, Bill	1972-73	2	0	0	0	0	11
Holt, Randy	1980-81 to 1981-82	56	0	5	5	174	7
Housley, Phil	1994-95 to 1995-96 & 1998-99 to 2000-01	328	50	188	238	140	6
Houston, Ken	1975-76 to 1981-82	462	128	145	273	516	24, 6
Hrdina, Jiri	1987-88 to 1990-91	157	36	58	94	63	17
Hull, Brett	1985-86 to 1987-88	57	27	24	51	12	16
Hulse, Cale	1995-96 to 1999-00	265	10	42	52	429	29, 32
Hunter, Mark	1988-89 to 1990-91	133	34	26	60	358	22
Hunter, Tim	1981-82 to 1991-92	545	49	59	108	2405	19
Huscroft, Jamie	1995-96 to 1996-97	109	3	13	16	279	7
Iginla, Jarome	1995-96 to 2003-04	626	250	253	503	422	24, 12
Ingarfield, Earl Jr.	1979-80 to 1980-81	17	2	3	5	6	21
Jackson, Jim	1982-83 to 1984-85	107	15	30	45	20	16
Jalonen, Kari	1982-83 to 1983-84	34	9	6	15	4	21
Jantunen, Marko	1996-97	3	0	0	0	0	45
Johansson, Andreas	1999-00	28	3	7	10	14	21
Johansson, Mathias	2002-03	46	4	5	9	12	20
Johansson, Roger	1989-90 to 1990-91 & 1992-93	150	8	34	42	157	21, 34

Player	Seasons	Games Played	Goals	Assists	Points	Penalty Minutes	Jersey No.
Johnson, Terry	1985-86	24	1	4	5	71	6
Karpenko, Igor	1998-99	-	-	-	-	-	29
Kea, Ed	1973-74 to 1978-79	316	22	92	114	283	24, 19
Keczmer, Dan	1993-94 to 1995-96	98	3	23	26	72	39
Kennedy, Sheldon	1994-95 to 1995-96	71	10	15	25	81	23
Ketter, Kerry	1972-73	41	0	2	2	58	24
Kidd, Trevor	1991-92 to 1996-97	123	0	9	9	26	37
Kiprusoff, Miikka	2003-04	38	0	1	1	15	34
Kisio, Kelly	1993-94 to 1994-95	63	14	27	41	34	11
Kobasew, Chuck	2002-03 to 2003-04	93	10	13	23	59	7
Kohn, Ladislav	1995-96 to 1997-98 & 2002-03	12	1	2	3	4	46, 43
Konroyd, Steve	1980-81 to 1985-86 & 1994-95	350	18	83	101	386	3, 7
Korn, Jim	1989-90	9	0	2	2	26	26
Kravchuk, Igor	2000-01 to 2001-02	115	4	30	34	23	25
Krivokrasov, Sergei	1999-00	12	1	10	11	4	17, 25
Kromm, Richard	1983-84 to 1985-86	189	43	61	104	90	22
Kruse, Paul	1990-91 to 1996-97	246	24	29	53	614	18, 12
Kryskow, Dave	1975-76	79	15	25	40	65	8, 20
Kyte, Jim	1990-91 to 1991-92	63	0	10	10	260	4
Labraaten, Dan	1980-81 to 1981-82	70	19	19	38	19	21
Lalonde, Bobby	1977-78 to 1979-80 & 1981-82	155	38	56	94	54	7, 11
Lakovic, Sasha	1996-97	19	0	1	1	54	38
Lamb, Mark	1985-86	1	0	0	0	0	16
Landry, Eric	1997-98 to 1998-99	15	1	1	2	4	11, 26
Lapointe, Claude	1995-96	32	4	5	9	20	47
Larose, Guy	1993-94	7	0	1	1	4	42
Laurence, Red	1978-79	59	14	20	34	6	17
Lavallee, Kevin	1980-81 to 1982-83	212	66	65	131	63	15
Lebeau, Patrick	1992-93	1	0	0	0	0	38
Leeman, Gary	1991-92 to 1992-93	59	11	12	23	37	11
Leiter, Bobby	1972-73 to 1974-75	234	64	81	145	41	16
Lemelin, Rejean	1978-79 to 1986-87	324	0	15	15	53	1, 31
Lemieux, Jean	1973-74 to 1975-76	140	10	38	48	35	20, 6
Lemieux, Jocelyn	1995-96	20	4	4	8	10	45
Lemieux, Richard	1975-76	1	0	1	1	0	20
Leopold, Jordan	2002-03 to 2003-04	140	13	34	47	36	4
Lessard, Rick	1988-89 & 1990-91	7	0	2	2	2	3, 32
Letang, Alan	2001-02	2	0	0	0	0	2
Lever, Don	1979-80 to 1981-82	113	48	58	106	66	12, 9
Lindberg, Chris	1991-92 to 1992-93	79	11	17	28	35	32, 11
Lindsay, Bill	1999-00 to 2000-01	132	9	21	30	183	22
Lombardi, Matthew	2003-04	79	16	13	29	32	49, 18
Loob, Hakan	1983-84 to 1988-89	450	193	236	429	189	12
Lowry, Dave	2000-01 to 2003-04	193	31	38	69	131	10
Loyns, Lynn	2003-04	12	0	2	2	2	20
Lydman, Toni	2000-01 to 2003-04	289	19	74	93	140	32
Lysiak, Tom	1973-74 to 1978-79	445	155	276	431	329	12
MacInnis, Al	1981-82 to 1993-94	803	213	609	822	944	11, 22, 2
MacLellan, Brian	1988-89 to 1990-91	134	35	35	70	95	27
MacMillan, Bill	1972-73	78	10	15	25	52	20
MacMillan, Bob	1977-78 to 1981-82	308	122	173	295	111	11
Macoun, Jamie	1982-83 to 1991-92	586	62	184	246	664	34
Makarov, Sergei	1989-90 to 1992-93	297	94	198	292	199	42
Malgunas, Stewart	1999-00	4	0	1	1	2	34
Manery, Randy	1972-73 to 1976-77	377	30	142	172	242	7
Markwart, Nevin	1991-92	10	2	1	3	25	23
Marsh, Brad	1978-79 to 1981-82	257	3	41	44	317	5, 22
Martineau, Don	1973-74	4	0	0	0	2	24

QUOTABLE

SERGEI MAKAROV ON ONE OF THE THINGS HE LIKED ABOUT BEING A MEMBER OF THE FLAMES:

"I'd heard about the rivalry. I knew that games between Edmonton Oilers and Calgary Flames were very exciting and very hard to play."

Digits at the 'Dome

397: The most goals the team scored in one season (1987-88.)

QUOTABLE

JIM PEPLINSKI ON

RETIRING FROM HOCKEY

AND THE FLAMES:

"I look at today as kind of

a graduation day. It's time

to hang up the blades and

move on and take all the

things I learned from

hockey and apply them to

a new endeavour. I just

hope it offers me the same

challenges that hockey

has and it leaves me with

the same great memories."

Player	Seasons	Games Played	Goals	Assists	Points	Penalty Minutes	Jersey No.
Matteau, Stephane	1990-91 to 1991-92	82	16	19	35	112	23
May, Alan	1994-95	7	1	2	3	13	41
McAdam, Gary	1981-82	46	12	15	27	18	28
McAmmond, Dean	2001-02 to 2003-04	137	38	43	81	78	37
McCarthy, Sandy	1993-94 to 1997-98	276	30	25	55	730	15
McCreary, Keith	1972-73 to 1974-75	231	49	50	99	91	9
McCrimmon, Brad	1987-88 to 1989-90	231	16	67	83	274	4
McDonald, Lanny	1981-82 to 1988-89	492	215	191	406	408	9
McDonough, Al	1973-74	35	10	9	19	15	14
McInnis, Marty	1996-97 to 1998-99	91	23	30	53	42	18
McKendry, Alex	1980-81	36	3	6	9	19	26
McLennan, Jamie	2002-03 to 2003-04	48	0	1	1	18	33, 29
McTavish, Dale	1996-97	9	1	2	3	2	41
Meehan, Gerry	1974-75 to 1975-76	62	11	30	41	8	10
Mercredi, Vic	1974-75	2	0	0	0	0	10
Meredith, Greg	1980-81 & 1982-83	36	6	4	10	8	29, 25
Millen, Corey	1995-96 to 1996-97	92	15	25	40	42	34
Miller, Brad	1993-94	8	0	1	1	14	55, 34
Mohns, Doug	1973-74	28	0	3	3	10	2
Mokosak, Carl	1981-82 to 1982-83	42	7	7	14	87	19, 10
Montador, Steve	2001-02 to 2003-04	87	3	5	8	190	58, 5
Morgan, Jason	2003-04	13	0	2	2	2	46
Morris, Derek	1997-98 to 2001-02	343	34	129	163	385	53
Morrison, Lew	1972-73 to 1973-74	130	7	13	20	19	8
Morrow, Scott	1994-95	4	0	0	0	0	27
Moss, Tyler	1997-98 to 1998-99	17	0	1	1	0	30
Mottau, Mike	2002-03	4	0	0	0	0	36
Mrozik, Rick	2002-03	2	0	0	0	0	51
Mulhern, Richard	1975-76 to 1978-79	207	25	67	92	153	4
Mullen, Joe	1985-86 to 1989-90	345	190	198	388	95	7
Murdoch, Bob	1978-79 to 1981-82	262	16	63	79	202	20
Murray, Bob	1973-74 to 1974-75	104	3	6	9	56	23
Murray, Marty	1995-96 to 2000-01	26	3	3	6	6	45, 28, 20
Murzyn, Dana	1987-88 to 1990-91	201	16	39	55	404	5
Musil, Frank	1990-91 to 1994-95	335	18	45	63	505	3
Muzzatti, Jason	1992-93 to 1994-95	2	0	0	0	0	31, 36
Myre, Phil	1972-73 to 1977-78	211	0	5	5	23	1
Nattress, Ric	1987-88 to 1991-92	226	9	53	62	204	6
Nazarov, Andrei	1998-99 to 1999-00	112	15	31	46	108	62
Nichol, Scott	2001-02 to 2002-03	128	13	14	27	256	40
Nieckar, Barry	1994-95	3	0	0	0	12	28
Niedermayer, Rob	2001-02 to 2002-03	111	14	24	38	91	44
Nieuwendyk, Joe	1986-87 to 1994-95	577	314	302	616	330	18, 25
Nieminen, Ville	2003-04	19	3	5	8	18	24
Nilson, Marcus	2003-04	14	5	0	5	14	26
Nilsson, Kent	1979-80 to 1984-85	425	229	333	562	90	14
Norwood, Lee	1993-94	16	0	1	1	16	6
Nylander, Michael	1993-94 to 1995-96 &1997-98 to 1998-99	168	34	74	108	54	92, 26
O'Flaherty, Gerry	1978-79	1	1	0	1	2	18
Oliwa, Krzysztof	2003-04	65	3	2	5	247	33
Olsen, Darryl	1991-92	1	0	0	0	0	32
Osiecki, Mark	1991-92	50	2	7	9	24	55
O'Sullivan, Chris	1996-97 to 1998-99	49	2	11	13	14	19
Otto, Joel	1984-85 to 1994-95	730	167	261	428	1642	29
Pankewicz, Greg	1998-99	17	0	3	3	20	33
Paradise, Bob	1972-73 to 1973-74	89	1	8	9	116	6
Paslawski, Greg	1992-93 to 1993-94	28	6	5	11	2	23
Patrick, James	1993-94 to 1997-98	217	14	56	70	82	6, 5, 3

Player	Seasons	Games Played	Goals	Assists	Points	Penalty Minutes	Jersey No.
Patterson, Colin	1983-84 to 1990-91	416	88	99	187	187	11
Peluso, Mike	1997-98	23	0	0	0	113	8
Peplinski, Jim	1980-81 to 1989-90 & 1994-95	711	161	263	424	1467	24
Petit, Michel	1991-92 to 1993-94	134	8	40	48	243	7
Petrovicky, Ronald	2000-01 to 2001-02	107	9	12	21	139	36
Phillipoff, Harold	1977-78 to 1978-79	118	26	53	79	241	24
Picard, Noel	1972-73	57	1	10	11	53	22
Plager, Bill	1972-73	76	2	11	13	92	2
Plett, Willi	1975-76 to 1981-82	452	150	149	299	1267	22, 25
Priakin, Sergei	1988-89 to 1990-91	46	3	8	11	2	16
Price, Noel	1972-73 to 1974-75	199	5	40	45	160	4
Pronovost, Jean	1978-79 to 1979-80	155	52	58	110	42	9
Quinn, Dan	1983-84 to 1986-87	222	72	119	191	100	10
Quinn, Pat	1972-73 to 1976-77	374	12	87	99	555	3
Racine, Yves	1996-97	46	1	15	16	24	36
Ramage, Rob	1987-88 to 1988-89	80	4	19	23	193	55
Ranheim, Paul	1988-89 to 1993-94	354	94	100	194	105	26, 28
Rautakallio, Pekka	1979-80 to 1981-82	235	33	121	154	122	4
Redmond, Dick	1977-78	42	7	11	18	16	5
Reese, Jeff	1991-92 to 1993-94	39	0	5	5	16	35
Regehr, Robyn	1999-00 to 2003-04	363	12	42	54	370	38
Reichel, Robert	1990-91 to 1996-97	425	153	201	354	217	26
Reierson, Dave	1988-89	2	0	0	0	2	8
Reinhart, Paul	1979-80 to 1987-88	517	109	335	444	203	23
Reinprecht, Steve	2003-04	44	7	22	29	4	27
Ribble, Pat	1976-77 to 1978-79 &1981-82 to 1982-83	203	12	31	43	188	23, 3, 22,8, 28
Richard, Jacques	1972-73 to 1974-75	215	57	46	103	108	15
Riggin, Pat	1979-80 to 1981-82	119	0	6	6	11	31, 1
Rioux, Pierre	1982-83	14	1	2	3	4	32
Risebrough, Doug	1982-83 to 1986-87	247	68	101	169	583	8
Roberts, Gary	1986-87 to 1995-96	585	257	248	505	1736	32, 10
Roche, Dave	1998-99 to 1999-00	38	3	3	6	49	25
Rochefort, Leon	1972-73 to 1973-74	110	19	30	49	23	11
Roloson, Dwayne	1996-97 to 1997-98	70	0	4	4	12	30
Romanchych, Larry	1972-73 to 1976-77	288	68	95	163	100	21, 9
Rota, Darcy	1978-79 to 1979-80	57	19	13	32	70	18
Russell, Phil	1978-79 to 1982-83	322	29	103	132	469	2, 3, 5
St. Sauveur, Claude	1975-76	79	24	24	48	23	11
Sabourin, Dany	2003-04	4	0	1	1	0	50
Sabourin, Ken	1988-89 to 1990-91	27	1	4	5	72	23, 55
Saprykin, Oleg	1999-00 to 2003-04	187	29	47	76	132	19
Sarault, Yves	1995-96	11	2	1	3	4	36
Savard, Marc	1999-00 to 2001-02	221	60	94	154	158	27
Schlegel, Brad	1993-94	26	1	6	7	4	21
Schulte, Paxton	1996-97	1	0	0	0	2	35
Scoville, Darrel	1999-00	6	0	0	0	2	2, 4, 45
Seiling, Rod	1978-79	36	0	4	4	12	15
Shand, Dave	1976-77 to 1979-80	288	14	63	77	324	8
Shannon, Darryl	1999-00	27	1	8	9	22	2
Shantz, Jeff	1998-99 to 2001-02	256	33	53	86	151	11
Sharples, Scott	1991-92	1	0	0	0	0	1
Sheehy, Neil	1983-84 to 1987-88 & 1991-92	222	13	34	47	725	5, 15
Simard, Martin	1990-91 to 1991-92	37	1	5	6	172	38, 13
Simon, Chris	2003-04	13	3	2	5	25	15
Simpson, Bobby	1976-77 to 1980-81	127	23	18	41	94	11, 22
Simpson, Todd	1995-96 to 1998-99	214	4	26	30	500	40, 27
Skalde, Jarrod	1995-96	1	0	0	0	0	38
Skrudland, Brian	1992-93	16	2	4	6	10	39

QUOTABLE

ROBYN REGEHR ON SIGNING A FIVE-YEAR CONTRACT WITH THE FLAMES IN 2003:

"I continue to believe I will improve. Last year, I thought I played consistently for most of the season, a pretty strong season. But I think I still have a lot more to offer."

Digits at the 'Dome

54: The most wins the Flames ever had in one season (1988-89.) The most losses, 41, came in 1996-97 and 1997-98.

QUOTABLE

MIKE VERNON ON

HIS UP AND DOWN

RELATIONSHIP

WITH FANS:

"You are either the

star or the goat."

Player	Seasons	Games Played	Goals	Assists	Points	Penalty Minutes	Jersey No.
Sloan, Blake	2001-02 to 2002-03	74	2	10	12	32	24
Smith, Brad	1979-80 to 1980-81	49	7	4	11	69	24, 18
Smith, Steve	1998-99 to 2000-01	102	1	20	21	139	55
Smyth, Greg	1991-92 to 1992-93	42	2	3	5	110	6
Sonnenberg, Martin	2003-04	5	0	0	0	2	25
Sorochan, Lee	1998-99 to 1999-00	3	0	0	0	0	33, 32
Stefaniw, Morris	1972-73	13	1	1	2	2	19
Stern, Ron	1990-91 to 1997-98	396	59	66	125	1288	22
Stewart, John	1972-73 to 1973-74	142	35	32	67	71	17
Stiles, Tony	1983-84	30	2	7	9	20	21
Stillman, Cory	1994-95 to 2000-01	393	109	126	235	192	20, 16
St. Louis, Martin	1998-99 to 1999-00	69	4	16	20	32	46, 15
Struch, David	1993-94	4	0	0	0	4	33
Sullivan, Mike	1993-94 to 1996-97	205	20	28	48	54	32
Sundblad, Niklas	1995-96	2	0	0	0	0	35
Suter, Gary	1985-86 to 1993-94	617	128	437	565	872	20
Sutter, Ron	2000-01	21	1	3	4	12	20
Sweeney, Bob	1995-96	6	1	1	2	6	17
Sweeney, Tim	1990-91 to 1991-92	53	8	11	19	12	7
Tabaracci, Rick	1994-95 to 1996-97 & 1997-98	97	0	4	4	22	31
Talafous, Dean	1974-75	18	1	4	5	13	24
Tambellini, Steve	1983-84 to 1984-85	120	34	20	54	20	15
Thompson, Rocky	1997-98 to 1998-99	15	0	0	0	86	55,22
Titov, German	1993-94 to 1997-98	345	107	121	228	142	13
Tkaczuk, Daniel	2000-01	19	4	7	11	14	18
Tonelli, John	1985-86 to 1987-88	161	40	76	116	164	27
Torgaev, Pavel	1995-96 & 1999-00	50	6	12	18	18	35, 18, 50
Trefilov, Andrei	1992-93 to 1994-95 & 1998-99	23	0	0	0	6	1, 35
Turek, Roman	2001-02 to 2003-04	152	0	10	10	18	1
Turnbull, Randy	1981-82	1	0	0	0	2	22
Unger, Garry	1979-80	79	17	16	33	39	17, 7
Vail, Eric	1973-74 to 1981-82	539	206	246	452	246	22, 25, 27
Varlamov, Sergei	1997-98 & 1999-00	8	3	0	3	0	24, 37
Vernon, Mike	82-83 to 83-84, 85-86 to 93-94 & 00-01 to 01-02	526	0	34	34	192	30, 29
Viitakoski, Vesa	1993-94 to 1995-96	23	2	4	6	8	32, 19
Volcan, Mickey	1983-84	19	1	4	5	18	5
Walker, Howard	1982-83	3	0	0	0	7	12
Walz, Wes	1993-94 to 1994-95	92	17	39	56	27	17
Wamsley, Rick	1987-88 to 1991-92	111	0	2	2	12	31
Wappel, Gord	1979-80 to 1981-82	20	1	1	2	10	24, 2, 21
Ward, Ed	1994-95 to 1998-99	215	16	24	40	284	42
Warrener, Rhett	2003-04	77	3	14	17	97	44
Werenka, Brad	1999-00 to 2000-01	45	2	5	7	37	33, 2
Whitmore, Kay	2001-02	1	0	0	0	0	35
Wiemer, Jason	1997-98 to 2000-01	219	33	30	63	502	24
Wilm, Clarke	1998-99 to 2001-02	303	31	42	73	250	23
Wilson, Bert	1980-81	50	5	7	12	94	8
Wilson, Carey	1983-84 to 1987-88 & 1990-91 to 1992-93	355	102	161	263	160	33
Wilson, Rik	1985-86	2	0	0	0	0	32
Wortman, Kevin	1993-94	5	0	0	0	2	34
Wregget, Ken	1998-99	27	0	1	1	8	31
Wright, Jamie	2001-02 to 2002-03	63	6	14	20	32	18
Yawney, Trent	1991-92 to 1995-96	274	11	45	56	368	18, 8
Yelle, Stephane	2002-03 to 2003-04	135	14	28	42	74	11
Young, C.J.	1992-93	28	3	2	5	20	23
Zaharko, Miles	1977-78	71	1	19	20	26	23
Zalapski, Zarley	1993-94 to 1997-98	178	21	55	76	220	33
Zemlak, Richard	1991-92	5	0	1	1	42	21

MacNeil

Crisp

Johnson

Head Coaches of the Calgary Flames

Al MacNeil 1980-82
Bob Johnson 1982-87
Terry Crisp 1987-90
Doug Risebrough 1990-91
Doug Risebrough and Guy Charron 1991-92
Dave King 1992-95
Pierre Page 1995-97
Brian Sutter 1997-00
Don Hay and Greg Gilbert 2000-01
Greg Gilbert 2001-02
Greg Gilbert, Al MacNeil and Darryl Sutter 2002-03
Darryl Sutter 2003 - present

Risebrough

Charron

King

Page

B. Sutter

Hay

Gilbert

D. Sutter

QUOTABLE

AL MACNEIL ON MOVING FROM COACHING TO AN EXECUTIVE ROLE WITH THE FLAMES IN 1982:

"I think we're not far away from becoming a powerful franchise . . . There's great potential here."

QUOTABLE

DARRYL SUTTER ON ADDING THE ROLE OF GENERAL MANAGER TO HIS DUTIES AS HEAD COACH IN 2003:

"It doubles my commitment. I have a huge responsibility to ownership, an unbelievable responsibility to fans . . . (and) a tremendous responsibility to our players. I know it's a big challenge, but I'm big-time ready for it."

fans

Flames Fandemonium

Flames car flags were everywhere during the playoff run in 2004 and became the hottest team souvenir, with stores selling out of large shipments in hours.

By VALERIE FORTNEY

It was the year thousands of newcomers learned what it means to be a true Calgarian.

Thanks to a pack of hardscrabble hockey players, the city and its citizens came together in 2004 in a show of world-class community spirit.

Several blocks of 17th Avenue S.W. became known as the Red Mile and the central party zone for tens of thousands of Flames fans, as the team took a run at the Stanley Cup in 2004.

The Calgary Flames' run to the 2004 Stanley Cup Final was torn from the pages of a modern-day fairy tale. And the good people of Calgary became a big part of that story, with their early excitement building up to a fan fanaticism phenomenon suitable for bedtime reading.

Its beginnings were evident during the Flames' first series against the Vancouver Canucks. Cars everywhere sprouted flags with the flaming C logo; team jersey-wearing school kids held up "Go Flames Go!" signs at recess; local radio stations created Flames songs; and babies sported curly red wigs in honour of player Mike Commodore's wild mane. And when the players started growing their scratchy playoff beards, so too did legions of couch potato male fans.

By the time our sporting underdogs beat the much-favoured Detroit Red Wings in round two of the playoffs, the city was in a state of scarlet frenzy. There was no better example of this than the now world-renowned Red Mile. Inner-city 17th Avenue S.W. became party central, with at times up to 60,000

red-shirted revellers filling the street, which was blocked off to cars. Fans hoisted everything in the air — homemade tin-foil Stanley Cups; children with red C's painted on their faces; and, of course, legions of signs, such as "You Gave Us Kiprusoff, Now You Get Summer Off," which was a nod to round-three losers San Jose Sharks.

The world took notice, partly because of some young women who, in a moment of misguided team spirit, shed those red shirts for the multitudes and the TV cameras. Photos and video of their bare chests appeared on Internet sites around the world. But more importantly, the Red Mile became the focus of worldwide attention because of the city's mass display of contagious sports enthusiasm which was, for the most part, peaceful.

What many of Calgary's newcomers didn't know, however, was that this wasn't the first time Flames fan frenzy overtook our city. In fact, over the years, Flames fans have surprised us more than once with their fervour.

Calgarians couldn't wait for the Flames to come to town and team souvenirs, shown here at the Corral on opening night (Oct. 9, 1980), quickly became a must-have item.

Fans rejoiced as the Flames continued to make the playoffs throughout the 1980s, but still waited for their hockey heroes to win the ultimate prize — the Stanley Cup.

As we commemorate a quarter-century of Calgary Flames action in our city, a nod to previous bouts of "fandemonium" — moments that hint at our Red Mile future — is only fitting.

Think it's tough getting Flames tickets in the 21st century? Try 1980 on for size. Mere minutes after the May press conference announcing the Flames were coming to town, the Calgary Exhibition and Stampede office was reportedly besieged by thousands of fans wanting to be first in line for tickets.

Fans were quick to rejoice when the Flames were hot, such as in the spring of 1986 when the Flames beat the Edmonton Oilers in the Smythe Division final. Thousands of fans poured into the streets to celebrate (above), especially on Electric Avenue, 11th Avenue S.W. (left.)

"Pinch me, I can't believe this is happening," said the late, great sports announcer Ed Whalen on the eve of the Calgary Flames' first NHL game. The next night, Oct. 9 to be precise, the sold-out crowd of about 7,000 in the old Corral at Stampede Park was hoarse from screaming, their feet sore from stomping, as the new hockey team took on the Quebec Nordiques.

Then-owner Nelson Skalbania hadn't anticipated the instant fan fever he was igniting. A few months earlier, he had riled thousands of hockey fans, with 15,000 having put deposits on the inaugural season's tickets in a 6,500-seat arena. "I never expected this to happen," a beleaguered Skalbania told the *Calgary Herald* in May of 1980 as he tried to explain how he pre-sold the arena by more than double its capacity.

Much to the fans' delight, the team made the playoffs during its first season in Calgary and Flames fever began to spread. On the afternoon of April 12, 1981, 500 fans descended on the Calgary International Airport to welcome the Flames, fresh from a thrilling double-overtime victory over the Chicago Blackhawks in Round 1 of the 1981 NHL playoffs. Even after the team lost to the Minnesota North Stars in the semifinal, the boys nicknamed "Calgary's Cinderfellas" were given a rock star-worthy reception by no less than 1,500 screaming fans when they landed at the airport at 2 a.m. "We're number one! We're number one! The Cup in '82!" chanted the boisterous crowd.

By the mid-1980s, the Flames were so hot that some enterprising season ticket holders were taking out newspaper ads and charging thousands of dollars for the rights to their much-coveted seats. At the games, excited fans would show up wearing red, giving birth to the Sea of Red we're so familiar with at the Pengrowth Saddledome today.

As Flames Fever burned across Calgary in 1986, even city aldermen, Don Hartman and Les Pears, took on the persona of the most beloved Flame of the time, the moustached Lanny McDonald.

In 1986, at the height of the Battle of Alberta — the long time rivalry between the Flames and Edmonton Oilers — hundreds of red-shirted Calgary fans bused, drove and flew north on a pilgrimage to the Edmonton Coliseum, as the famed adversaries met once again in the playoffs. Fans back home did their part in the frenzy. Adults filled the streets and pubs to celebrate, while kids at local schools dressed in red and held up their Flames banners in the schoolyards.

We loved our Flames, and boy, did we love our Flames captain, Lanny McDonald. During the playoffs, fake Lanny moustaches were the ultimate Flames fan accessory; even Calgary City Hall got into the act, with aldermen showing their team spirit by sporting the faux 'staches in the usually staid council chambers.

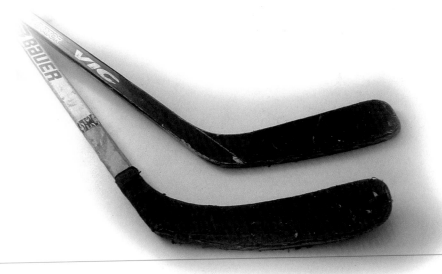

Back then, the Flames were once again the underdogs. It was Oilers superstar Wayne Gretzky's best year, as he set records for both assists (163) and points (215). But unlike the previous season, in which the Oilers dowsed the Flames after seven stressful games, this time it was the Oilers' turn to cry.

Upon their victorious return to Calgary, the hockey team was witness to an overwhelming, unprecedented show of fan adoration. Star goalie Mike Vernon and his fellow players were greeted at the airport by no less than 10,000 hugging, hollering and hooting fans. (Some in attendance even claim the number was closer to 25,000). "It was pandemonium," one *Herald* writer said at the time, noting the lines of people at the fence at the airport were 30 metres deep, while late-arrivers continued arriving to welcome back their team.

That year, with every playoff win, a growing number of fans descended on Electric Avenue, the former nightclub strip along 11th Avenue S.W. But Electric Avenue would have to wait three more years for the big party: the Flames were stopped short of their Stanley Cup dream by the Montreal Canadiens in Game 5 of the final playoffs.

When the Flames captured the Stanley Cup in 1989, fans poured into Calgary Streets — including party central at the time, Electric Avenue — to celebrate the win.

97

A parade held to celebrate the Stanley Cup win in 1989 attracted tens of thousands of people into Calgary's downtown.

The 1989 Stanley Cup parade was a pivotal point for Flames fans, who had waited since the team's arrival in 1980 to see the cup in Calgary.

However, on May 25, 1989, our boys exacted revenge for that 1986 loss, beating the Canadiens and bringing the Stanley Cup to Cowtown for the first time. On that jubilant night, more than 30,000 fans jammed the seven-block long Electric Avenue in a show of open air fan devotion the city had never before seen. Nearby, the Calgary Tower lit a 4.3-metre-high flame in celebration of the team's win.

Over the next 14 seasons, the Flames' playoff runs were short — and even non-existent in eight of those seasons. The fans weren't as boisterous in those years, but many stayed loyal. That loyalty was rewarded during the 2004 NHL playoffs. The flame atop the Calgary Tower once again burned brightly — and for much longer than anyone had ever dared to hope.

Despite coming so close to victory against the Tampa Bay Lightning, in 2004 our Cinderella hockey team fell one game short of returning the Stanley Cup to Calgary. But that loss didn't stop fans from showing their love for the team: when the down and dejected players arrived at the Calgary Airport in the wee hours of June 8, 2004, 1,000 of the devoted were on hand to offer support. "Sorry we couldn't do this for you guys," was all that the normally gregarious Ken King, the Flames' CEO and president, could say on the players' behalf.

As the team entered its 25th anniversary season of hockey action in Calgary in 2005, it was no surprise that game tickets were again almost as scarce as they were in 1980. Fans, the memories of 2004 still fresh, were determined to once again show their true colours as they cheered on the boys. And once again, more newcomers were looking forward to the experience of knowing what it means to be a true Calgarian. After all, the Calgary Flames have been showing us how for the better part of 25 years.

Fans threw themselves into the excitement of the 2004 playoff games, turning the Saddledome into the Sea of Red.

In 2004, Flames playoff excitement swept the city, especially as thousands of kids participated in organized and spontaneous fan rallies.

The faces of Flames fans helped electrify the 2004 playoff run.

The Red Mile, along 17th Avenue S.W., became the gathering place for thousands of fans during and after every 2004 playoff game. It captured the attention of North America as it became well known not only for its massive parties, but for its girls-gone-wild atmosphere.

Fans continued to show their support for the Flames after the team lost the Stanley Cup Final in 2004. Hundreds turned up at the airport to meet the team as they arrived home, where fan favourite Mike Commodore stopped to sign autographs. "I love these fans," said the then-Flames defenceman. "They are a big part of this and they've had a tough night, too. You won't find support like this anywhere else in the world."

About 30,000 people attended a rally for the team two days after the 2004 Cup loss to the Tampa Bay Lightning, with Jarome Iginla telling the fans, "This is truly unbelievable. You guys helped make this year and this run the time of our lives. We couldn't ask more from our fans, and if there's any question, it is not even close who the best sports fans are in the world. This has been an unbelievable ride."

Outskate, Outshoot, Outscore

Over the past 25 years, the Flames have produced many hockey heroes who have dazzled us with their skating, shooting and puck-stopping abilities. A wide variety of players have become fan favourites over the years, but some players' names come up regularly whenever anyone starts discussing the greatest Flames of all time. Here are 15 of those hockey stars.

KENT NILSSON 1979-80 to 1984-85

He frustrated defencemen, baffled goaltenders, amazed teammates and sometimes infuriated coaches. But most of all, Kent Nilsson dazzled fans.

Known as The Magic Man during his five seasons with the Calgary Flames and one campaign with the Atlanta Flames, the smooth-skating Swede made an immediate impact on fans when he scored 49 goals and 82 assists in the 1980-81 season, the team's first in Calgary. Those 131 points, which is still a club record, left him third in the league in scoring, just behind Marcel Dionne of the Los Angeles Kings and Edmonton's Wayne Gretzky.

Nilsson's natural ability even drew compliments from Gretzky, who called Nilsson one of the most talented players in the world. Nilsson's teammates couldn't argue.

"In my opinion, Kenta (the nickname Nilsson carried) was as good as the guy 200 miles north (Wayne Gretzky) — when he wanted to play," Nilsson's onetime linemate Ken Houston once said. "Willi Plett and I would joke about it. We'd say, 'Get the puck to the Swede and go to the net with your stick on the ice and it's usually going to end up in the net.' "

The slick centreman proved to be a dominating force in his years in Calgary, scoring 189 goals and 280 assists in just 345 games. He had another 40 goals and 53 assists when the team was based in Atlanta.

But in a lot of ways, many were left wondering if he ever reached his true potential.

While his Magic Man label was partly due to his magnificence with the puck, it also referred to his on-ice disappearing act. He could turn defencemen inside out or deke goalies out of their Fruit of the Looms, but when he didn't feel like giving it his all, he was invisible.

"That was the talent I didn't have," says Nilsson. "Talent is stick-handling or play-making, but you have the talent of drive, too, and maybe that was the talent I didn't have."

To his coaches, solving the Rubik's Cube was easier than figuring out the No. 14 puzzle.

"Coaching Kenta was a joy in a lot of ways," said Al MacNeil, who coached Nilsson for two seasons. "In other ways, it would drive you bananas. He was an absolute enigma."

Despite scoring 37 goals and 62 assists in the 1984-85 season, Nilsson took heat for the team's playoff failure and was traded to the Minnesota North Stars in exchange for two draft picks. One of those two players turned out to be Joe Nieuwendyk — who had a great career of his own in Flames colours.

After two seasons in Minnesota, Nilsson wrapped up his career playing parts of two seasons with Edmonton, where he now works as a scout.

— DALE OVIATT

Kent "Magic Man" Nilsson was the first star who emerged with the Calgary Flames, netting a team record of 131 points in a single season.

LANNY McDONALD 1981-82 to 1988-89

In Calgary, the Flames franchise was fresh, barely a year old and the first NHL season in the city had brought about a surprisingly decent result — a march all the way to the Stanley Cup's final four. But now the Flames knew they needed something else. A face.

Enter Lanny King McDonald. In November 1981, the Flames sent everyday forwards Bob MacMillan and Don Lever to the Colorado Rockies in exchange for The Moustache.

"I know the players traded away were popular and I'm not going to try to replace them," McDonald had said that day. "I hope the fans take to me the way they took to them."
Rest assured, they did.

McDonald was an Alberta boy. He'd been raised in Hanna, played Junior A in Lethbridge and played major junior in Medicine Hat. And now he was returning to Alberta. He'd never leave.

"My first thought was, 'Oh my gosh, Colorado didn't want me.' But you forget that there's another team out there that obviously wanted you and that's why they traded for you," says McDonald. "I felt a lot of pressure coming back so close to home and family and friends. It really turned out to be a blessing and it was the best thing that ever happened for my career."

McDonald, then only 28 years old, encompassed key components of leadership — he was gritty, skilled and outgoing. In his first 55 games with the Flames, the charismatic right-winger triggered 34 goals.

Then came the 1982-83 campaign.

McDonald did the impossible, chasing Wayne Gretzky from the start of the season to its bitter end in the race for goal production. By the time the dust had settled, McDonald, with his snappy wristshot and patented wraparound, had produced 66 goals. Gretzky — 71.

But more than individual sprees, the Flames were dying for team success. They made it to the Stanley Cup Final in 1986, but fell to the Montreal Canadiens.

Three years later, they were back. They didn't fail this time, wrenching the Cup away from the Canadiens, thanks to a tally from you-know-who, ol' No. 9.

"I scored my first goal ever in the National Hockey League in the Montreal Forum. And I scored my last goal in my final game, again, in the Montreal Forum," says McDonald. "I was part of the on-ice lineup for that winning game and we were the only team, other than the Canadiens, to ever win the Stanley Cup on Forum ice. All those things added up to me thinking, 'Boy, it's a sign. It's time I was out of here.' What a great way to go."

Eight years earlier, on the day he landed on the Flames doorstep, McDonald had been asked about being a winner. "This team has the potential to be a winner," said McDonald, who would wear the captain's 'C' from 1983 to 1989, "and I'm not ready to retire for quite a while yet."

When he did, it was with a Stanley Cup ring and nearly 600 games of service for his beloved Flames.

"If you want to be good inside and outside the rink, Mac's a good guy to pattern yourself after," former teammate Jim Peplinski once said. "He's first-class all the way."

— SCOTT CRUICKSHANK

Lanny McDonald celebrates his 1,000th point, scored on March 7, 1989.

Al MacInnis's ultra-
powerful slapshot was a
thing of beauty to fans.

AL MacINNIS 1981-82 to 1993-94

The legend of Al MacInnis was born on Jan. 17, 1984. That was the night the rifleman from Port Hood, N.S., cranked up from outside the blue line and unleashed a sizzling shot that cracked St. Louis Blues netminder Mike Liut's mask and trickled into the net.

MacInnis would go on to terrorize opposition goalies — not to mention defencemen and the rare, brave shot-blocking forward — for the next two decades.

One of the most cannonading shooters in NHL history, the man known as Chopper would hit the 20-goal plateau seven times in his stellar career, with six of those big years coming in Calgary colours.

With 1,274 points, a Norris Trophy and seven all-star team berths on his resume, it's hard to recall MacInnis's early struggles to hone and refine his considerable talents. The former Kitchener Rangers junior standout had to overcome the fact he wasn't a naturally fluid skater and develop the instincts of knowing precisely when to unleash his booming slapper.

The lessons were quickly learned — he rattled off big point totals yearly from the mid-'80s to the early-'90s, with staggering career highs of 28 goals, 75 assists and 103 points in 1990-91.

MacInnis was one-half of some of the greatest one-two blue-line tandems in NHL history; with Scott Stevens in junior, with Gary Suter in Calgary and with Chris Pronger in St. Louis. He was an intelligent player, a sure puck handler and a supreme power-play quarterback. But, any discussion about the all-star inevitably went back to The Shot.

"You try to squeeze a little more Charmin in the pads when you face him," once remarked former Red Wings goaltender Kevin Hodson, speaking for his puck-blocking brethren.

"One time," recalled Oilers goalie Bill Ranford, "Al hit me on the end of my thumb and it was like somebody had grabbed my bare hand and slammed the car door on it over and over. I can't describe the pain . . . and it wasn't even broken. He is

the only guy who can hit you in the middle of your glove, where there is plenty of padding, and it still stings. It's scary."

The big shooter played a huge role in the Flames' Stanley Cup triumph in 1989, racking up 31 points in 22 games and earning the Conn Smythe Trophy as the most valuable player in the playoffs.

Traded to St. Louis in 1994, MacInnis continued his exceptional play and remained among the league elite at an age when others' skills deteriorated. He was named the NHL's best defenceman at age 35 and earned first-team all-star honours at 39. When he retired in September 2005, it was largely because of an eye injury that had kept him sidelined for almost an entire season.

"Nobody played the game and prepared like Al," noted former Flames coach and assistant GM Al MacNeil. "His off-ice conditioning and training for games was second to none. He was the best conditioned defenceman in the NHL . . . and that is one of the reasons why he was so good."

MacInnis won ardent admirers for more than his on-ice production.

"Probably the nicest thing that I can say about a hockey player that I've met and coached," said Terry Crisp, Calgary's bench boss when the Flames won the Cup in '89, "is what I can say about Al MacInnis: He is a class act, both on and off the ice. Probably one of the best ambassadors the game of hockey has ever had."

— JEAN LEFEBVRE

JAMIE MACOUN 1982-83 to 1991-92

Jamie Macoun may have been under-rated as a defenceman, but was in fact a solid contributor to the Flames.

Too many people remember Jamie Macoun for all the wrong reasons. To be sure, the defenceman was involved in more than his fair share of notorious incidents during his 17-year career.

He cracked one of Winnipeg Jets star Dale Hawerchuk's ribs during the 1985 playoffs. He was on the receiving end of a devastating sucker punch from brutish Edmonton Oilers centreman Mark Messier. His high stick resulted in a broken jaw for Buffalo Sabres dandy Pat LaFontaine.

But for those who were really paying attention — like his teammates, for instance — Macoun was an integral if too-often overlooked member of the talented Flames teams of the late '80s and early '90s.

"I think he was one of the most under-rated defenceman of that era," says longtime teammate Jim Peplinski.

Thanks to their offensive prowess, Al MacInnis and Gary Suter were the Calgary blue-liners who grabbed most of the headlines. Brad McCrimmon was probably the meanest of the Flames' back-line bunch. That left the solid and steady Macoun to quietly and efficiently go about his work.

Though best classified as a stay-at-home rearguard, Macoun nevertheless recorded at least 30 points in each of his first four NHL campaigns.

Macoun twice overcame long odds to play in the big leagues. To begin with, he played at Ohio State, a football factory but hardly a hockey hothouse in the early '80s. Undrafted, Macoun instead signed a free-agent deal with Calgary. The former Buckeye quickly rewarded the Flames' faith in him by earning a spot on the NHL's all-star rookie team in 1983-84.

Then, in 1987, his career seemingly came to a horrifying halt when an automobile accident left him with extensive nerve damage in his arm. The long, arduous recovery and rehabilitation process forced him to miss the entire 1987-88 season, but he returned to play a valuable role in the Flames' 1989 Cup championship.

Remarkably, he would play 11 seasons after the career-threatening mishap. He added a second Stanley Cup ring in 1998 as a member of the Detroit Red Wings.

Macoun concluded his career in 1999 with 76 goals, 358 points and 1,208 penalty minutes in 1,128 games for Calgary, Toronto and Detroit. He added 159 post-season appearances. Although he left the city in 1992 in what many Flames fans feel is the worst deal in franchise history — Macoun, Doug Gilmour, Ric Nattress, Kent Manderville and Rick Wamsley went to the Leafs in return for Gary Leeman, Alexander Godynyuk, Jeff Reese, Michel Petit and Craig Berube — the Newmarket, Ont., native settled in Calgary after hanging up his skates.

— JEAN LEFEBVRE

MIKE VERNON 1982-83 to 1983-84;
1985-86 to 1993-94; 2000-01 to 2001-02

Even at the height of his game in Calgary, local debate raged over goalie Mike Vernon and his net-minding abilities.

But after a 17-year National Hockey League career, his accomplishments end up speaking for themselves. Vernon was the kid from southwest Calgary who made it to the big time; the first Flames goaltender who wasn't intimidated by the Edmonton Oiler juggernaut of the mid-1980s.

Vernon led the Flame franchise to its first, and extremely unlikely, berth in the 1986 Stanley Cup Final as a spring call-up from Salt Lake City.

Three years later, he backstopped the club to win Lord Stanley's silver mug during a rematch with the Montreal Canadiens — and, in the process, became one of only four goalies in NHL history to beat the Habs in a Cup final.

But instead of a local-boy-makes-good tale, there often seemed to be a "love-hate relationship" between Vernon and Calgary's hockey-mad citizenry.

"You've got to have a pretty thick skin to play goal," Vernon once remarked. "Fans at hockey games get very emotional. They're very passionate. They don't enjoy watching their team give up goals."

In September 2002, Vernon finally hung up his mask and trapper, following a long and fruitful NHL career with Calgary, Detroit, San Jose, Florida and finally Calgary again. After winning the Stanley Cup with Calgary, he played in two more Cup finals; drank from the silver chalice once more with Detroit in 1997; and finally hoisted that Conn Smythe Trophy as a Red Wing, winner of the playoffs' MVP title — a title which some felt he should have earned with the '89 Flames.

In June 2005, when Vernon went up for induction into the Hockey Hall of Fame for the first time, confident and authoritative voices proclaimed Vernon one of the very best of his era.

"There's one thing that is always overlooked with Mike," offered mastermind coach Scotty Bowman. "He beat Patrick Roy head-to-head in two big playoff series — once with Calgary and once with us in Detroit. How many other goalies can make that claim?"

Seventh in all-time NHL regular-season wins with 385, Vernon also finishes fourth among goalies in all-time playoff appearances (138), and fifth in all-time playoff victories (77). "In his era," says NHL goalie-turned-broadcaster John Garrett, "he and Patrick and Grant Fuhr were heads and shoulders above everyone else at the position." Adds Mr. Goalie, Glenn Hall: "I always thought Grant Fuhr was the best goalie of his time. But I always thought Vernie was very close."

The upshot? Even a local lightning rod like Mike Vernon has found that you can go home again.

"I've had good numbers ever since I left Calgary," he said near the end of his playing days. "(It makes) people kind of realize that, 'You know what? Maybe he is a good goaltender.'"

— TODD KIMBERLEY

Goalie Mike Vernon was key in the Flames' success in the 1989 Stanley Cup playoffs.

HAKAN LOOB 1983-84 to 1988-89

With five hat trick games under his belt in 1987-88, Hakan Loob holds the team record (along with Theo Fleury) for most three-goal games in a single season.

His stature — short and Swede.
His stay — short and Swede.
His impact — far and wide.

When Hakan Loob arrived in Calgary in 1983, no one really knew what to expect. Maybe the numbers — five foot nine, 170 pounds, 181st overall pick in 1980 — would tell the story.

Not even close.

The shifty right-winger, cloaked in No. 12, stayed around only six seasons, but became the first Swede to reach the 50-goal mark (in 1987-88). That was thanks, in part, to a franchise-record five hat tricks and a trip to the 1989 Stanley Cup that capped his quickie pro career.

"Once I told Calgary I was going home, I got a great offer from Cliff Fletcher. I could have written a pretty good deal with Calgary at that time," says Loob, looking back. "But my wife (Marie) and I made a decision fairly early, almost a year before we went home, and it was based on the social life of the family." (Their sons Henrik and Niclas were 8 and 4, respectively at the time.)

"But even now, I don't second-guess myself. The decision was right for us at the time. We never regretted it."

By the time the classy winger packed up, the ink dried on an NHL resume that included 450 regular-season games with 429 points, and 73 playoffs games with 54 points.

"Just landing at Calgary airport was unbelievable to me — to get a chance to prove I could play in the NHL," says Loob. "A lot of people told me it wouldn't be possible, with the size I had."

His new teammates soon learned what Loob was about. He became a member of the 1984 all-star rookie team, with his 30 goals that season. "He didn't fight, he didn't hit, but he was tough," says Perry Berezan. "Smooth as he was, he never played soft."

Adds another former teammate, Jim Peplinski: "Many people overlooked what Loob brought to our team. A tremendous skater, a competitor — he wouldn't score when you were up by three goals, he'd score when you were down by one." And he was unafraid to walk away on top. Not many players win a Stanley Cup. None retires in his prime immediately after doing so.

"It meant quite a bit because it's considered the biggest achievement ever in hockey, but for me, personally, some Swedes had done it before," says Loob of the 1989 championship, in which he contributed 17 points in 22 games. "When I went back (home), it wasn't like there was a parade or anything like that, so you don't get a balloon head."

Across the Atlantic Ocean, Loob watched in stunned joy when his former squad made its run in the spring of 2004. Years and time zones removed from the heat of battle, he still felt it. "It doesn't matter if none of the players are still there from my day, or if most of the people in the organization have moved on," says Loob. "When you go through what we did — two months of sacrifice to win the Stanley Cup together — the city and the team always stay in your heart. It's a bond that cannot be broken."

— SCOTT CRUICKSHANK

JOEL OTTO 1984-85 to 1994-95

It's not an insult. It's reality.

To talk about the greatness of Joel Otto, you must also talk about the greatness of Mark Messier.

Addressing the former is to address the latter.

The signature snapshot of Otto through his decade-plus in Calgary silks isn't an end-to-end rush, nor is it a nose-bending scrap, a blurring slapshot or a board-rattling check.

Rather it was Otto — all six foot four and 220 pounds of him — wearing that familiar No. 29 sweater, continually tugging at the front of it, then bending from the waist, lower and lower until he'd halved his height and he was ready.

For a faceoff.

Against Messier.

A key cast member in the Battle of Alberta in the 1980s when it was at its bloodiest and its nastiest, Otto was singled out to get in the way of Messier of the Edmonton Oilers. Most pros of that era would rather have eaten bees than go head-to-head with Messier, but Otto did, literally.

"The big centreman was just becoming popular then — Messier probably inspired that — and Calgary didn't have a lot of those type of players," says Otto. "In a way, he's responsible for me being in the league."

Otto did the job of taking on Messier very well. So well, in fact, that when the Philadelphia Flyers got tired of getting kicked in the teeth by Messier, they summoned Otto as a big-buck free agent. Messier was by then with the New York Rangers and the feud began anew.

"I respected him. Did I like him? I'm sure he's a wonderful man, but . . . Well, there wasn't a lot of idle chit-chat between us. A few swear words, I guess. But I owe him my career in a way," says Otto. "So they (the Flames) gave me a try, because they had to find somebody to try and match Messier physically. Obviously, I couldn't match him skill-wise. For me, every game against him was a big thing. For him? Probably not. He had someone like me facing him every time he stepped on the ice."

On Flames teams brimming with talent — other pivots included Joe Nieuwendyk, Doug Gilmour and Theo Fleury — Otto's offensive contributions may have been overlooked. But who scored the Game 7 overtime goal against the Vancouver Canucks in 1989? Joel Otto. In fact, in that run to the Stanley Cup, Otto collected 19 points in 22 games. Nine times, he scored 13 or more goals in a season. He gave Calgary more than 800 games, regular- and post-season, nearly 500 points and 1,800 penalty minutes.

All this for a guy from Elk River, Minn.; a guy who played four unheralded winters for the NCAA Bemidji State Beavers; a guy who was never drafted.

"I went out on my own terms," says Otto, who retired after the 1997-98 campaign. "And I got a heck of a lot more out of my career than anybody expected. Not bad for a kid from from small-town Minnesota. As far as my career goes, everything came up roses."

— SCOTT CRUICKSHANK

The well-liked centre Joel Otto played more than 800 games for the Flames.

117

JOE MULLEN 1985-86 to 1989-90

Joe Mullen's stats easily reserved him a glass showcase at the Hockey Hall of Fame.

Joe Mullen was a player who never said quit.

But it was more than skill that led him from the streets of Hell's Kitchen, N.Y., where he played roller hockey, to pro hockey. There was also determination — and an immeasurable amount of heart — that made him one of the top players for 16 NHL seasons.

"Mully spent a career excelling in areas of the ice a lot of guys wouldn't visit on a threat of death," former teammate and Flames assistant coach Brad McCrimmon once said. "Great balance on his skates. Great desire. Great teammate. A little guy with big talent and a huge heart."

Of course, that heart of a lion was part of a complete package, which included a pretty good set of hands that came with that pint-sized five-foot-nine, 180-pound frame.

From the day the right-winger was acquired from the St. Louis Blues on Feb. 1, 1986, he became a fan favourite. It was more than the 16 goals and 22 assists he tallied in his 29 games the rest of that 1985-86 season. It was the grit, guts and offensive touch he added in the playoffs, leading all playoff scorers with 12 goals and guiding the Flames to the Stanley Cup Final against the Montreal Canadiens.

Over the next four seasons, he was as consistent as any scorer in the NHL, firing 47, 40, 51 and 36 goals. Twice he led the Flames in scoring (1986-87 and 1988-89), and twice brought home post-season silverware in the way of the Lady Byng Trophy as the league's most gentlemanly player. He was second in team scoring in the Flames' 1989 Stanley Cup championship run, sniping 16 goals in 21 games.

"I tried to give it 100 per cent and play both ends of the rink," says Mullen. "I tried to concentrate on my defensive side of my game. Once we turned it over and we had the puck, it was all-out offensive. Get the puck to the centre and try to get in the open, get it back and shoot."

No matter the score, Mullen never took a night off. "He goes where the heavy going is, comes in front of the net and is smart enough to know how to take a check," former Flames coach Terry Crisp once said. "A lot of players give you a first effort and that's it. With Mully, you'll see a second and third and sometimes even a fourth effort where he scores from his knees. He simply refuses to accept the fact they are trying to take him out of the play."

Mullen was traded in 1990 for a second-round draft pick to the Pittsburgh Penguins, where he went on to win two more Stanley Cups in five seasons. After one season in Boston, Mullen returned to Pittsburgh for a final season. He retired in 1997 with 502 goals and 561 assists, earning him induction into the Hall of Fame in 2000. He is now an assistant coach with the Penguins.

— DALE OVIATT

GARY SUTER 1985-86 to 1993-94

Gary Suter joined the Flames family with very little fanfare. The University of Wisconsin defenceman was chosen in the late going of the 1984 draft — after being passed over the two previous years — long after the stud prospects are invited to come on stage to model new sweaters and just before the cleaning crew moves in to sweep up.

Suter, who was back home in Madison working in a beer factory when his name was called by the Flames, admits he was less than thrilled by the news.

"Actually, when I heard I'd been drafted," said Suter, "I was kind of bummed out. Initially, anyway. That was the year, remember, when all those free agents — the Adam Oateses and Ray Staszaks — were happily signing wherever they wanted to go. I was really hoping to go that route. Then I got picked and it was like 'Oh . . . yeah? . . . Great . . .'

"I remember the Flames sent me a jersey with a No. 9 on it. And I thought, 'What gives? Have they traded Lanny McDonald?' He was the only Flame I knew, I'd ever heard of, at that time. I was confused. 'Why are they giving me his number?'

"Turns out the 9 was for the round I'd been drafted in." That deep in the draft, Suter remarks, "teams are usually wasting picks." But there was nothing throwaway about the steal of Suter, however. Rarely has a team made a better late investment.

Less than two years after being drafted, Suter was handed the Calder Trophy as the NHL's top rookie.

For eight and a half seasons in Flames colours, Suter was one of the best blue-liners in all of the NHL, even if he was somewhat overshadowed on his own club by the presence of Al MacInnis.

Six times during his Flames career, he recorded seasons of 60 points or better, highlighted by a spectacular 1987-88 campaign — 21 goals and 70 assists. With 437 assists, Suter ranks third on the Flames' all-time list and he's fourth in overall points with 565.

The Flames' 1989 Stanley Cup championship was a bittersweet experience for Suter. A broken jaw suffered in the first round sidelined Suter for the remainder of the playoffs and he wasn't in uniform the night the Flames hoisted the Cup over their heads at the Montreal Forum.

After leaving Calgary, Suter continued his distinguished career with the Chicago Blackhawks — where he played with close pal and former Wisconsin teammate Chris Chelios — and then San Jose, where he became a favourite of then Sharks skipper Darryl Sutter.

Suter's retirement prior to the 2002-03 season was one of the explanations for the slow start by the Sharks, which led to Sutter's firing. Shortly thereafter, Sutter was hired by the Flames.

"Sutes had a great career," says coach Sutter. "He won a Stanley Cup, he was an all-star and he has been a great role model for our young players."

— JEAN LEFEBVRE

Gary Suter ranks fourth on the Flames' all-time points list.

GARY ROBERTS 1986-87 to 1995-96

There was the retirement. There were tears. There was the league award in honour of his National Hockey League career.

But to those closest to Gary Roberts, it was no surprise there was also a comeback. His wife, Tamra, can pinpoint exactly when she knew Roberts would make a return: It was just three hours after an operation on his neck, "When he said, 'Drop the puck.'"

Roberts, the whippersnapper from Whitby, Ont., will probably go down in team history as the most gritty, talented and ultimately courageous skater to ever wear the Flaming C. He'd had eight notable seasons in the NHL, when bone spurs and disc degeneration in his neck became such a problem that he couldn't take a two-pound dumbbell in his left arm and lift it above his shoulder.

The six-foot-one, 190-pound left-winger was faced with a long, arduous road to recovery, especially if he hoped to play hockey again. In March 1995, and again in October of that year, Roberts put his future in the hands of Dr. Robert Watkins, opting for microscopic cervical surgery on the

left side of his neck at the Kerlan-Jobe Orthopaedic Clinic in Los Angeles.

It worked. And on Jan. 10, 1996, Roberts returned to the Flames' lineup — and to a standing ovation at the Saddledome. During his electric performance against the Hartford Whalers that night, Roberts' tally sheet went something like this: one goal, two penalties, a half-dozen bodychecks, and a cross-check across the neck from Jeff Brown that caused no ill effects. All in the first period. The team had 35 games left in the season and Roberts' comeback resulted in a gutsy 22-goal, 42-point tally for him. Roberts' inspirational tale earned him the '95-96 Bill Masterton Memorial Trophy, presented annually by the NHL for dedication, perseverance and sportsmanship. At the end of that season, however, neck problems forced Roberts to announce his retirement.

"If you want to play hard . . . your career is going to be short," Roberts said at the time. "I'm not bitter with anybody. I've taken some hits that should have been penalties. But I had to be there in front of the net (where) I scored my goals."
As it turns out, Roberts' NHL career has been anything but short. After retiring and spending the entire '96-97 campaign away from the rink, he made yet another comeback — this time with the Carolina Hurricanes, after the Flames traded him a few weeks prior to 1997 training camp.
At the start of the '05-06 season, Roberts was 39 and in his first season with the Florida Panthers — his 18th season in the league — after scoring 83 goals over four seasons with the Toronto Maple Leafs.

A participant in the '92 and '93 all-star games, Roberts is only the second player in NHL history to score 50 goals while also piling up 200 penalty minutes in a single season, turning that trick with the Flames in '91-92.

— TODD KIMBERLEY

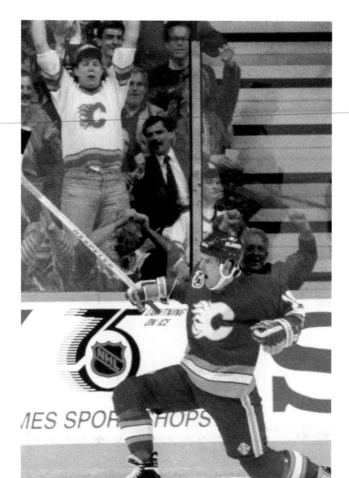

Gary Roberts made headlines after successfully returning to hockey following neck injuries and surgeries.

JOE NIEUWENDYK 1986-87 to 1994-95

He was chosen with a draft pick acquired from the Minnesota North Stars, in exchange for the enigmatic but immensely gifted centreman Kent Nilsson. He was a little-known Cornell University skater called Joe Nieuwendyk, but when he first arrived in Calgary the kid with the hard-to-say and harder-to-spell name was better known as 'Joe Who?'

By the end of his second season at the Saddledome, teammates, fans, media — and certainly opposition netminders — knew exactly who this fellow was. No ordinary Joe, he fired 51 goals in each of his first two campaigns. The first season was followed by his selection as NHL rookie of the year, while the second was capped by Calgary's capture of the Stanley Cup.

"We were both 23 at the time," recalls Gary Roberts, Nieuwendyk's childhood friend and NHL teammate in Calgary, Toronto and Florida. "I remember we looked at each other and said, 'Wow, that was pretty easy.'"

Roberts and Nieuwendyk played both hockey and lacrosse together as youngsters in Whitby, Ont. "We used to call him Crazy Legs because he could skate like the wind," says Roberts. "But he wasn't very big. He took a lot of abuse as a younger guy. Other teams would say, 'Get rid of Nieuwendyk and we can win.'

"When he went to Cornell he was a 165-pound runt. When he came back, he was 195 pounds and four inches taller." says Roberts. The all-grown-up centreman was one of the young stars — along with Roberts and Theoren Fleury — who beautifully blended with the Calgary veterans in the late '80s, as the powerful Flames won a Cup and back-to-back Presidents' Trophies as the NHL's top regular-season outfit.

On Jan. 11, 1989, Nieuwendyk enjoyed the best single night by a Flames goal scorer, potting five goals in an 8-3 victory over the Winnipeg Jets. Nieuwendyk played eight seasons for Calgary and is second on the franchise's all-time goal list with 314 tallies.

Even in leaving the Flames after a contract holdout in 1995, Nieuwendyk's contributions to the club continued. Part of the return from the Dallas Stars for Nieuwendyk's rights was a

junior winger by the name of Jarome Iginla. Proving that things come full circle, the immediate reaction in some corners of Calgary was 'Jarome Who?'

Precisely a decade after his Cup win with Calgary, Nieuwendyk added a second ring as a member of the Stars. A key cog he was, too, scoring six game-winners in the playoffs and being voted the winner of the Conn Smythe Trophy as most valuable player in the post-season. Cup No. 3 came in 2003, by which time Nieuwendyk was skating with the New Jersey Devils.

Though injuries have dogged him throughout his career, the son of Dutch immigrants has achieved all of the magic career milestones — 1,000 games, 500 goals, 500 assists and 1,000 points.

— JEAN LEFEBVRE

Joe Nieuwendyk scored more goals (five) in one game than any other Flames player ever has.

THEOREN FLEURY 1988-89 to 1998-99

He was one of the smallest players in Flames history. One of the most controversial, too. And colourful, gifted, accomplished, fiery, determined . . . There simply aren't enough adjectives in the dictionary to describe the life and times of Theoren Fleury.

The darkest chapters in Fleury's NHL life came after Calgary, turbulent times as a member of the New York Rangers. By comparison, his days with the Flames were relatively happy and carefree, not to mention prolific.

By the time Fleury and the Flames parted ways in 1999, the mighty mite from Russell, Man., was the franchise's all-time leader in goals (364) and points (830). He was also second in assists (460) and games played (791). He's up there in penalty minutes, too — his 1,339-minute tally is fifth most in club history.

Flames fans loved to see Fleury celebrating his goals, as he became one of the team's biggest stars.

A remarkable legacy for a pint-sized winger who more than one scout firmly believed would never skate a shift in the NHL.

At five foot six, Fleury was considered too wee to stand up to bruising big-leaguers. That's why, in spite of a 61-goal, 129-point season with the Western Hockey League's Moose Jaw Warriors, he lasted all the way to the eighth round of the 1987 draft — the 166th overall selection — before the Flames rolled the dice.

"Well, my size always was my biggest obstacle," concedes Fleury when asked about the stature issue. "From early on, even when I played in Moose Jaw, I had to play a certain style of game in order to get room on the ice. It's obvious the way teams draft players and what-not nowadays, they like big guys. When you're a smaller guy, you definitely have to make room for yourself and show that you are not going to be intimidated on the ice."

The dynamo made his NHL debut on Jan. 3, 1989 and wasted little time showing up the skeptics. He recorded his first point — an assist — a game later and his first goal — against Edmonton's Grant Fuhr, no less — in the game after that. He finished the season with 34 points in 36 contests and had a hand in the Flames' drive to the Stanley Cup championship, recording five goals and six assists. That would set the tone for his career — the guy who supposedly couldn't cut it became a point-a-game producer for the duration of his 1,084-game NHL stint.

Same deal in the hot and heavy action of the playoffs, where he produced 79 points in 77 games. One of Fleury's playoff goals led to one of the most famous images in Flames history — his exuberant sliding, arm-pumping celebration of an overtime winner in Game 6 of a 1991 playoff encounter with the hated Edmonton Oilers.

"When you use the word 'little' to describe Theo Fleury you're not talking about his heart," Wayne Gretzky once said, hand-picking Fleury to play for Canada at the Salt Lake City Olympics. "This is a 50-goal scorer who could play for any team in the NHL. He's a small man who has the ability to make the big play at any time. He's living proof that size is not an insurmountable hurdle in making it to the NHL. I thoroughly enjoyed playing with Theo in the Canada Cup (in 1991). His quickness in going to the net often catches defencemen and goaltenders asleep. When his arms are raised after scoring a goal, then he doesn't look so small."

By the time Fleury finished his stormy career, he had amassed seven all-star game appearances, 455 goals and 633 assists for 1,088 points.

"I guess when you first come out of juniors," Fleury once said, "you just want to be a solid NHL player. And for me, I had the opportunity to play with some really great players along the way that have helped me."

— JEAN LEFEBVRE

DOUG GILMOUR 1988-89 to 1991-92

Off the ice, Doug Gilmour wasn't intimidating. Not even a bit. Officially listed at five foot 11, he was probably a couple inches south of that. The book said Gilmour tipped the Toledos at 175 pounds, but by the end of a gruelling season, the slight centreman struggled to keep his weight above 160.

On the ice, however, Gilmour was a giant. For Flames fans, the lingering image of the feisty pivot known as 'Killer' will always be his heavily stubbled face and the no-nonsense, almost glowering expression after scoring the winning goal in the 1989 Stanley Cup Final against the Montreal Canadiens. Calgary's one and only Cup conquest was the culmination of a long process and many events, but few dates were as critical as Sept. 6, 1988. That's the day Cliff Fletcher pilfered Gilmour from the St. Louis Blues (along with Mark Hunter, Steve Bozek and Michael Dark) in exchange for Mike Bullard, Craig Coxe and Tim Corkery.

The lion-hearted centreman would prove to be the final piece in Calgary's championship puzzle. He was great during the season — 85 points and a stunning plus-45 rating — and even better in the playoffs, with 11 goals including the Cup-clincher. So empty was Gilmour's tank by the end, that he didn't have the strength to parade the silver chalice around Montreal Forum ice. All-out was the only way the Kingston, Ont., native knew to play.

"With Killer," says former Flames goaltender Rick Wamsley, "it was kind of like the 'my-dad's-tougher-than-your-dad' skinny little kid in the playground thing. You hit him once, he had to hit you twice. You hit him 10 times, he had to hit you 11. You could knock him down and blacken his eye, but he wouldn't let it die until he'd hit you that one extra shot; until he'd won."

Gilmour spent his entire career proving people wrong. One of the few people who believed in him was Gord Wood, a Cornwall Royals scout who convinced the junior club to take a look at the scrawny teenager who was then a 150-pound defenceman.

"Dougie's small," Wood has said, "but he's got the biggest heart I've ever seen."

Converted to centre, Gilmour posted huge numbers for Cornwall, but the NHL remained skeptical — he was ignored his first draft year and lasted until the seventh round of his second before the Blues finally took the plunge.

"I think the reason why I play the way I do," Gilmour once told reporters, "is because everybody always said I was too small. So it's just something that motivates you. It's like, 'You know what? We'll see.'"

By the time he stopped making doubters look foolish, Gilmour had played 1,474 games for the Blues, Flames, Maple Leafs, Devils, Blackhawks, Sabres and Canadiens and recorded 450 goals and 1,414 points.

— JEAN LEFEBVRE

Doug Gilmour was integral in the Flames' capture of the Stanley Cup in 1989.

MIIKKA KIPRUSOFF 2003-04 to present

What was the absolute greatest season ever turned in by a member of the Calgary Flames?

Lanny McDonald's 66-goal campaign in 1982-83, you say? Does Kent Nilsson's 131-point effort in 1980-81 get your vote? Or how about defenceman Al MacInnis's 103-point year in 1990-91?

They're all spectacular accomplishments, to be sure, but all perhaps should take a back seat to the efforts of Miikka Kiprusoff in 2003-04, even though the netminder from Turku, Finland, appeared in fewer than half the Flames' games that winter.

Acquired from the San Jose Sharks on Nov. 16, 2003, in exchange for a second-round draft pick, Kiprusoff quickly became the single biggest difference between a club that would reach the Stanley Cup Final and the sorry squad that had sat out the post-season party the seven previous springs. All the remarkably unflappable, impossibly cool Kiprusoff did was post a 24-10-4 record and establish a modern-day NHL record with a miniscule 1.69 goals-against average. Despite the late break from the gate and six weeks missed because of a knee injury, Kiprusoff was a finalist for the Vezina Trophy as the league's top puckblocker. An incredible turn of events for a masked man who started the season as the Sharks' No. 3 netminder.

"I never thought that Miikka was a backup goaltender," says Sharks goaltending coach Warren Strelow. "I thought he had to be a No. 1 guy to play well. That's the way he is. When he gets into it, he gets confidence.

Miikka Kiprusoff set a modern-day NHL record with his 1.69 goals-against average in 2003-04.

"If I had been on the other side of the fence, I'd have taken him. Without a doubt. There wouldn't have been a question. I called Kipper the day after he got traded and I told him, 'Now here's your opportunity. This is what you've been waiting for. Take advantage of it . . . and don't be too good against San Jose.' "

Much to fans' delight, the pupil didn't listen to his former mentor — Kiprusoff backstopped the Flames to a six-game victory over the Sharks in the 2004 Western Conference final. "He's got good flexibility," assesses former Flames netminder Rick Wamsley. "Structurally, he's sound, (has) decent hands and he's become a big-save guy. You can just sense it in him."

"The thing about Kipper," says Flames netminding prospect Brent Krahn, "(is) you watch the way he plays, and everything to him is a simple save. He works hard to stop the puck, but from a spectator's standpoint, it looks like it was an easy save. A guy could be on a breakaway and he'll make a save and he makes it look like anybody off the street can make that save. I think he really gives his team that confidence, knowing that no challenge is too great. I think that comes from experience, I think that comes from knowledge of the game, knowledge of the position. I think that comes from poise and focus."

— JEAN LEFEBVRE

JAROME IGINLA 1995-96 to present

Jarome Iginla's not only a great scorer; he's also a big physical presence on ice.

Jarome Iginla's not only a great scorer; he's also a big physical presence on ice.

From the perspective of his present station — as one of the planet's finest hockey players — it's interesting to harken back, to rekindle those first moments of his professional career one decade ago and to out the doubters of Jarome Iginla. On that fateful day, Iginla had been jolted out of deep sleep to hear the news, so his ensuing confusion is understandable. Told that he'd been traded to Calgary, Iginla immediately thought that the Hitmen of the Western Hockey League had acquired him from the Kamloops Blazers. Which, in a way, made sense. He was, at that precise moment, attending the national junior team's camp in Moncton, N.B.

Iginla soon learned the truth of that December 1995 deal — that the Calgary Flames, shockingly, had acquired him by sending disgruntled star Joe Nieuwendyk to the Dallas Stars. "I guess maybe it's a little pressure," Iginla, then 18, had said of the trade. "But it's not a bad thing because it helps me work harder. It's exciting, too, because it means they have confidence in you."

Soon, however, the Flames were defending the move to critics: "There is no crapshoot," Calgary's interim general manager Al Coates said at the time. "We know what we are getting." Even if others did not.

"I don't mean to dismiss him," said Nieuwendyk. "I just don't know who he is."

The St. Louis Blues, in particular, were boiling mad at losing out on the Joe Nieuwendyk Sweepstakes and not being able to make a trade to acquire him. Huffed Brett Hull: "We offered more and other teams offered more (for Nieuwendyk) than what Calgary got. They got nothing. I've never seen a guy (Coates) offered nothing and accept it. What kind of commitment to winning is that?"

Added Al MacInnis: "I think what everyone else in the league thinks of it — not much. I don't know what Calgary was thinking. Was that the best deal on the table? Dallas didn't have to give up anything to get (Nieuwendyk)."

But the hockey world soon learned what the Flames had — and no one had to wait long. The afternoon following the Blazers' elimination from the WHL playoffs, Iginla made his NHL debut, joining the Flames in their post-season series against the Chicago Blackhawks. Two games, two points — just like that.

With 21 goals and 50 points the following season, Iginla made the NHL's 1997 all-star rookie team. After suffering a textbook sophomore jinx — 13 goals in 70 games — Iginla reeled off campaigns of 28, 29 and 31 goals.

Then came the career-altering winter of 2001-02. Olympic gold, 52 goals, Hart Trophy finalist, Lester B. Pearson Award winner. And, with 96 points, he became the first member of the Flames to lead the league in points. "I couldn't ask for more of a dream season, except for making the playoffs and winning the Stanley Cup," Iginla, still only 24, said at the time. "There are more dreams. But, I'll tell you, a lot of them have been delivered this year. Thanks be to God. It's mind-boggling to think of the things that I got to experience this year."

He experienced plenty more in 2003-04, holding down role of team captain, sharing the league lead for goals and, on his broad shoulders, carrying his Flames to Game 7 of the Stanley Cup Final.

Now, as the Flames leave their first quarter-century in Calgary, there are precious few doubters.

The Hockey News, no less, calls Iginla the No. 1 player in the NHL. There's the scoring touch, there's the toughness, there's the leadership. He's made the transition — from Jarome Who? . . . to Jarome, That's Who. His current pace will eventually carry him to the top of all the Flames' offensive charts.

"I remember when he got traded for Nieuwendyk and how it was outrage in the city. But they've come to embrace what a special player he is," says Flames winger Darren McCarty, a three-time winner of the Stanley Cup, who also notes the humble side of Iginla. "Like all the greats, he sort of ho-hums it. I've watched Steve Yzerman a lot of years, and that's the way he is. One thing you notice is that his source for energy is all from the positive side — the glass is half full. You really flock to guys who lead like that."

Not surprisingly, many of the rave reviews for Iginla come from his Calgary cohorts, the guys who spend the most time with him.

"He leads as a good friend, not as a parental figure. He leads as an equal," says Flames defenceman Andrew Ference. "He doesn't put himself on the pedestal, pump his chest and say, 'Everybody listen up because I'm the best player here.' He doesn't operate that way. I don't think it's in his nature. Guys can go talk to him . . . and there's not that intimidation, that superstar aura. You can have a two-way conversation, instead of a lecture."

— SCOTT CRUICKSHANK

PHOTOGRAPHY

Front Cover: Grant Black, *Herald*; Back cover: *Herald Archives*; Endsheets: Chad Persley, Calgary Flames; p.I Dean Bicknell, *Herald*; p.III Grant Black, *Herald*; p.4 Dean Bicknell, *Herald*; p.5 Ted Rhodes, *Herald*.

Chapter 1
p.6 *Herald Archives*; p.7 John Lightfoot; p.8 Dean Bicknell, *Herald* (Seaman), *Herald Archives* (Skalbania); p.9 Larry MacDougal, *Herald*; p.10 *Flames Archives*; p.12 Jacqueline Downey, *Herald* (top), Jenelle Schneider, *Herald* (bottom); p.13 *Herald Archives*; p.14 Ted Jacob, *Herald*; p.15 Jim Cochrane, *Edmonton Journal*; p.16 Marianne Helm, *Herald* (top), Dave Olecko, *Herald* (bottom); p.17 *Flames Archives*; p.18 Peter Battistoni, *Vancouver Sun* (Gelinas), John Lightfoot (helmet); p.19 Peter Battistoni, *Vancouver Sun*; p.20 Dean Bicknell, *Herald*; p.21 *Flames Archives*.

Chapter 2
p.22-25 *Herald Archives*; p.26 *Herald Archives* (Gretzky), Kim Stallknecht, *Herald* (Risebrough); p.27-28 *Herald Archives*; p.29 *Herald Archives* (Macoun), John Colville, *Herald* (Faceoff); p.30 Bruce Stotesbury, *Herald*; p.31 *Herald Archives*; p.32 John Skrypnyk, *Herald* (Suter), *Herald Archives* (Wilson), Larry MacDougal, *Herald* (Quinn); p.33 *Edmonton Journal* (Smith), *Herald Archives* (Vernon); p.34 Bill Herriot, *Herald* (fans), *Herald Archives* (Vernon, Hunter, trophy); p.35 Randy Fledler, *Herald* (sign), Ted Rhodes, *Herald* (banners); p.36 Larry MacDougal, *Herald* (McDonald), Dean Bicknell, *Herald* (Risebrough), Kim Stallknecht, *Herald* (Wilson); p.37 *Herald Archives*; p.38 Larry MacDougal, *Herald*; p.39 *Herald Archives* (Scuffle, Flames), Mike Fiala, *Herald* (Hull); p.40 Ray Smith, *Herald* (Mullen), *Herald Archives* (McDonald, Nieuwendyk, Hunter); p.41 Larry MacDougal, *Herald* (Macoun), *Herald Archives* (Crisp); p.42 *Herald Archives* (McDonald, Gilmour), Larry MacDougal, *Herald* (Vernon); p.43 *Herald Archives*; p.44 Larry MacDougal, *Herald* (McDonald), Bill Herriot, *Herald* (cup), *Herald Archives* (Hunter, Fleury); p.45 *Herald Archives*; p.46 Mike Sturk, *Herald* (Fleury), Dave Olecko, *Herald* (Patterson), David Lazarowych, *Herald* (Nieuwendyk); p.47 Dean Bicknell, *Herald* (Musil), Shannon Oatway, *Herald* (Stern); p.48-51 *Herald Archive*; p.52 Dean Bicknell, *Herald*; p.53 Dean Bicknell, *Herald* (MacInnis), Larry MacDougal, *Herald* (Kidd); p.54 Larry MacDougal, *Herald* (Fleury), *Herald Archives* (Bearcat), David Lazarowych, *Herald* (Roberts), Dave Olecko, *Herald* (Nieuwendyk); p.55 *Edmonton Journal* (brothers), Shannon Oatway, Herald (Featherstone), Dave Olecko, *Herald* (Iginla), Les Bazso, *Province* (Fleury); p.56 David Lazarowych, *Herald* (Simpson), Jeff McIntosh, *Herald* (Miss Canada), Larry MacDougal, *Herald* (McCarthy), Dave Olecko, *Herald* (Thompson); p.57 Mike Sturk, *Herald* (Fleury, Morris), Marianne Helm, *Herald* (Ward), David Moll, *Herald* (Fleury); p.58 Dean Bicknell, *Herald* (Fuhr), Chris Relke, *Herald* (Bure), Mike Sturk, *Herald* (Regehr), Marianne Helm, *Herald* (Flames); p.59 Grant Black, *Herald* (Vernon, Conroy), Keith Morison, *Herald* (Wiemer); p.60 Ted Jacob, *Herald* (Turek), Dean Bicknell, *Herald* (Whalen), Grant Black, *Herald* (Iginla); p.61 Leah Hennel, *Herald* (Sutter), Mikael Kjellstrom, *Herald* (Drury), Jenelle Schneider, *Herald* (Harvey); p.62 Peter Battistoni, *Vancouver Sun*; p.63 Peter Battistoni, *Vancouver Sun* (Kiprusoff), Ric Ernst, *Province* (Iginla); p.64 Grant Black; p.65 Colleen Kidd, *Herald* (Kiprusoff), Dean Bicknell, *Herald* (Flames), Grant Black, *Herald* (Iginla); p.66 Grant Black, *Herald* (Warrener), Ted Rhodes, *Herald* (Conroy), Dean Bicknell, *Herald* (Regehr, Montador, Commodore, Lowry, Nieminen), Marianne Helm, *Herald* (Donovan); p.67 Dean Bicknell, *Herald* (Flames), Grant Black, *Herald* (Montador), Mikael Kjellstrom, *Herald* (Iginla); p.68 *Herald Archives*; p.69 Dean Bicknell, *Herald* (Kiprusoff, Ference, Flames), Grant Black, *Herald* (Gelinas); p.70 Grant Black, *Herald* (Saddledome), Ted Rhodes, *Herald* (Sutter), Mikael Kjellstrom, *Herald* (Weimer); p.71 Jenelle Schneider, *Herald* (Warrener), Dean Bicknell, *Herald* (Simon), Stuart Gradon, *Herald* (banner).

Chapter 3
p.72 *Herald Archives*; p.74 John Lightfoot (sticks), Ric Ernst, *Province* (Iginla); p.75 Rob Galbraith, *Herald* (MacInnis), *Herald Archives* (Musil); p.76 Mike Fiala, *Herald* (Nieuwendyk), Ted Jacob (pucks); p.77 *Herald Archives*; p.78 Grant Black, *Herald*; p.79 Colleen Kidd, *Herald*; p.80 *Herald Archives*; p.81 Ted Rhodes, *Herald*; p.82-84 *Herald Archives*; p.85 Ted Rhodes, *Herald*; p.86 Keith Morison, *Herald*; p.87 Jenelle Schneider, *Herald* (MacNeil), Mike Fiala, *Herald* (Crisp), *Herald Archives* (Johnson, Risebrough, Charron, Sutter), Shannon Oatway, *Herald* (King), Rob Galbraith, *Herald* (Page), Mikael Kjellstrom, *Herald* (Hay), Grant Black, *Herald* (Gilbert), Dean Bicknell, *Herald* (Sutter).

Chapter 4
p.88 Jenelle Schneider, *Herald*; p.89 Randy Hill, *Herald* (flags); p.91 *Herald Archives* (souvenirs); Kim Stallknecht, *Herald* (Santa); p.92-93 *Herald Archives*; p.95 Dean Bicknell, *Herald*; p.96 John Lightfoot (sticks), Larry MacDougal, *Herald* (fans); p.97 Dean Bicknell, *Herald*; p.98-100 *Herald Archives*; p.101 Ted Jacob, *Herald*; p.102 Jenelle Schneider, *Herald* (fans), Dean Bicknell, *Herald* (Harvey); p.103 *Herald Archives*; p.104 Marianne Helm, *Herald* (top left), Jenelle Schneider, *Herald* (top right), Ted Rhodes, *Herald* (middle), Ted Jacob, *Herald* (bottom); p.105 Jenelle Schneider, *Herald*; p.106-107 Colleen Kidd, *Herald* (Commodore, rally), Jenelle Schneider, *Herald* (Iginla).

Chapter 5
p.108 *Flames Archives*; p.109 David Lazarowych, *Herald*; p.110 Tom Walker, *Herald*; p.111 *Flames Archives*; p.112 *Herald Archives*; p.113 David Lazarowych, *Herald*; p.114 *Herald Archives*; p.115 Mike Fiala, *Herald* (top), *Flames Archives* (bottom); p.116-117 *Flames Archives*; p.118-119 *Herald Archive*; p.120 *Flames Archive* (top), Dave Olecko, *Herald* (bottom); p.121-122 *Flames Archives*; p.123 Mike Fiala, *Herald*; p.124 *Flames Archives*; p.125 Mikael Kjellstrom, *Herald*; p.126-127 Ted Rhodes, *Herald*.

The following names have been shortened:
Flames: Calgary Flames
Herald: the Calgary Herald
Province: The Province (Vancouver)